THE ENDING OF THE WORDS
MAGICAL PHILOSOPHY OF ALEISTER CROWLEY

The Stele of Revealing 666

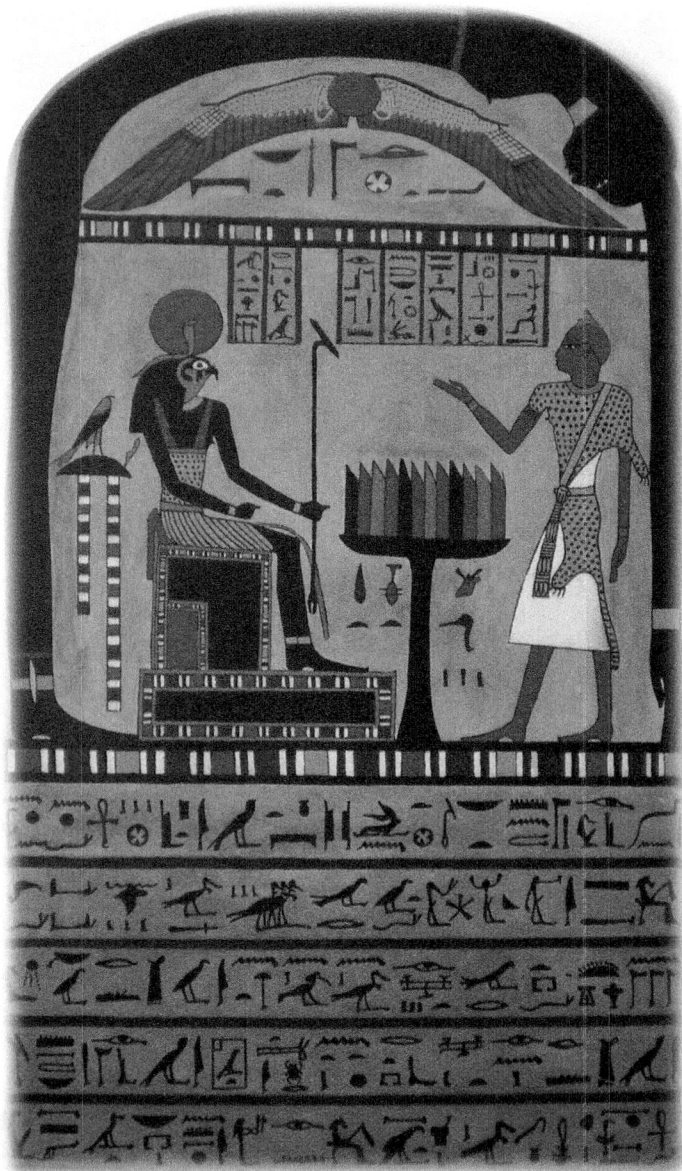

ORDO ASTRI

THE ENDING

OF THE

WORDS

MAGICAL PHILOSOPHY OF

ALEISTER CROWLEY

BY

OLIVER ST. JOHN & SOPHIE DI JORIO

ISBN 978-0-9559784-0-1

First Published 2007
Revised 2014, 2016

Photograph of *The Master Therion (Aleister Crowley the Beast 666)* from the oil painting by Leon Kennedy, with the kind permission of Tony Naylor, of Mandrake Press Ltd.

Photograph of *The Temptation of Saint Anthony* by Félicien Rops supplied by the Bibliothèque Royale de Belgique, Brussels.

ORDO ASTRI IMPRIMATUR
www.ordoastri.org

Other Books by Oliver St. John

The Ending of the Words—Magical Philosophy of Aleister Crowley

Hermetic Qabalah—A Foundation in the Art of Magick

Ritual Magick—The Rites and Ceremonies of Hermetic Light

Hermetic Qabalah Initiation Workbook

The Mystic Tarot and the Trees of Eternity

Magical Theurgy—Rituals of the Tarot

Hermetic Astrology

Dedication of a Sanctuary or Temple

In Preparation (2016):

The Flaming Sword Sepher Sephiroth

The Law of Thelema—Quantum Yoga

Contact the O∴ A∴

The O∴ A∴ is an Independent Thelemic School of the Mysteries with an operational collegium and grade system based on the Hermetic Tree of Life. Contact details and information on courses and membership availability is posted on the Ordo Astri website: www.ordoastri.org

Contents

Preface

Do what thou wilt shall be the whole of the Law.

Hermetic wisdom is not obtained by intellectual effort alone, since mystical symbolism alludes to that which is outside of time and space and therefore beyond the limits of the human reason. To prepare for the gnosis that may come through work and discipline it is necessary to organise and to inform the mind. Unless this is accomplished the person shall be ill fit to approach the source of all power and knowledge.

Liber AL vel Legis, the Egyptian Book of the Law, was communicated to Aleister Crowley (1875–1947) via the mediumship of his wife, Rose.[1] According to Crowley, the book proclaimed the advent of the Aeon of Horus. It was dictated in 1904 by a praeterhuman intelligence called Aiwaz. Named as the "minister of Hoor-paar-kraat" in the book, the work of Aiwaz was to reveal the law governing a new phase of human spiritual evolution, the Law of Thelema.

As minister of the God of Silence who presides over the eternal aeon *outside* of time, it was not the function of Aiwaz to manifest or to incarnate the New Aeon. A chaotic period in history of unprecedented proportions thus followed the transmission of the book. Before a magical aeon can be incarnated or fixed in time, the word or truth of the previous aeon must be broken down and assimilated. Only then may Horus achieve Maat—his full expression. The operation is directed by Ra Hoor Khuit, the active counterpart and twin of Hoor-paar-kraat, the god of Silence. Ra Hoor Khuit is a martial god of "Force and Fire" that embodies and manifests the power of Set or Saturn, the Lord of Time.

Through the ages, spiritual events are rooted in time. The evolution of man's deeper understanding of himself and the cosmos is anchored by historical events—whether these are understood as being 'real' or 'imagined'.

---

[1] Aleister Crowley numbered the manuscript "Liber XXX", a reference to the Qabalistic value of the letter "L" that was the original title of the book: Liber L vel Legis. The book is also known as Liber CCXX (220 verses) as well as by the 'corrected' number, XXXI. Crowley added an Aleph (A = 1) to the Lamed (L = 30), against the advice of I: 36: "My scribe Ankh-af-na-khonsu, the priest of the princes, shall not in one letter change this book." Ankh-af-na-khonsu was the name of all members of an Initiatic Theban cult.

The twelve equal divisions of the Great Year of the precession of the equinoxes may represent an historical age, for example. These are a little over 2000 years each. The Age of Aquarius is descriptive of the present time where the sunrise at the spring equinox now aligns with the constellation associated with Aquarius, the Waters of Space.[2] *Magical* aeons may take place in a thousand years or they may pass in a second—in the twinkling of an eye. They may also run concurrently with historical ages. Aleister Crowley suggested there are three historical aeons: Isis, Osiris and Horus. The Aeon of Isis represents a prehistoric time of matriarchy, where hunting and gathering predominated. Following this—after some considerable time—came the patriarchal Aeon of Osiris in which agriculture and civilisation flourished. The Aeon of Horus is then to be understood as the child of these parents, indicating a stage where individuals must take responsibility for their own actions.[3]

The subject of magical timing could warrant a whole book all to itself. According to some occultists, the magical Aeon of Horus as declared by Crowley was abortive and ended in 1948—a mere 44 years after the reception of Liber AL vel Legis. An Aeon of Maat then superseded the Aeon of Horus.[4] The notion here is that the Egyptian goddess Maat represents the perfection or completion of the Great Work or Hermetic Arcanum on earth. No aeon in *time* can truly be called "perfect" since all manifestation requires the continuous adjustment or balancing of *karma* or "actions in time". As Horus enters his Maatian phase—called Hrumachis in the book—the first result is necessarily polarisation and separation:

There is division hither homeward; there is a word not known. Spelling is defunct...

Liber AL vel Legis, III: 2

---

[2] The Aeon of Hrumachis mentioned in Liber AL vel Legis may be understood as the present Age of Aquarius where the four fixed or Kerubic signs of the Zodiac now dominate the precessional horoscope.

[3] Aleister Crowley's concept of three great Aeons does not concur with the precession of the equinoxes and twelve signs of the Zodiac, though Crowley, in a somewhat confused manner, attempts to assert that it does in his *The Book of Thoth or Egyptian Tarot*.

[4] A student and disciple of Aleister Crowley, Frater Achad (Stansfeld Jones), put forward the year 1948 as the beginning of an Aeon of Maat.

The spiritual power that initiated the Aeon of Hrumachis or Horus-Maat is a Mercurial, Setian intelligence or "star". The keys of the knowledge of heaven and hell, of life and death, have been passed on in the silence of an Aeon that is, as yet, little understood. The Law of Thelema is occult, "written and concealed", as stated in Liber AL vel Legis (III: 75). Man has failed to understand the runes that forecast his own doom.

The aim of this *Magical Philosophy* is to assist in establishing the enigmatic Law of Thelema in the context of the ages old Hermetic tradition from whence it emerged. The reception of the Book of the Law by Aleister Crowley in 1904 was not the first occasion in which the Word addressed a prophet; much of the language and symbolism of the book has its origin in the Egyptian and Judaeo Christian tradition. The language used in Liber AL vel Legis indicates that the book may best be understood as being rooted in a vastly ancient tradition of divine revelation. For example, the symbols of the "Beast" and the "Scarlet Woman" can be traced to the Apocalypse of St. John, the last book of the Christian New Testament. The "Abomination of Desolation", the special title of the Egyptian Stele that inspired the book, appears in both the New Testament and the book of Daniel in the Old Testament. St. John the Divine and the prophet Daniel are merely two better known cases of those who received direct revelation and transmitted this through their writings and work.

The doctrine typified in the Christian tradition by the assumption of the Virgin Mary predates the Christian era and is portrayed in the Thelemic tradition as the mystical saga of the Scarlet Woman or Soul. The magical principle of soul and body is referred to throughout this present volume as feminine ("she"; "her") while the principle of spirit and mind is treated as though masculine ("he"; "his"). This is a literary and poetic convention in the language of more than one mystic tradition. The legend of the Hero, Christ or Saviour who passes through trial and ordeal to be born in spirit reached its apotheosis at the Egyptian cult centre Aunnu, known by the Greeks as Heliopolis and called On in the biblical Old Testament. Here was celebrated the birth, death and resurrection of the hawk-headed star-god Horus. In Liber AL vel Legis, this god takes various forms. Among these are the Sphinx, the Dwarf Soul, and the Angel of Judgement.[5]

---

[5] Christ is often confused with Osiris. Whereas Osiris remained in the underworld as Lord of the Dead, Christ and Horus both ascended to heaven. "Heaven" and "paradise" (or Amentet) are two quite different worlds.

iv

The *Khabs*, the *Khu* and the *Ka* are ancient Egyptian pictographic symbols, and the many gods mentioned in Liber AL vel Legis are specific to the transformative roles played by deity at cult centres of Egypt such as Thebes and Heliopolis.

Liber AL vel Legis is scattered through with riddles requiring the use of the system known as the Qabalah to unravel. We have anticipated familiarity with the law of magical correspondences and the branch of Qabalah called Gematria. The general reader, though, should have little difficulty in following the lines of thought, since the rudiments of Gematria are very simple. In Greek and Hebrew, letters are numbers and numbers are letters. Words can therefore be added up to produce a number that represents the fundamental value of that word. Meaning may then be obtained from the relationship of words having the same numerical value. For example, the word "Thelema", "Will", adds to 93 by Greek Qabalah, as does "Agape", "Love". The "will" and "love" indicated by these words can be said to have identical or related meaning. The name of Aiwaz, the intelligence that transmitted the Book of the Law, is also Qabalistically equal to the number 93.

There is included here in the Appendices a full glossary of technical terms used in Liber AL vel Legis and elsewhere, plus some key historical references. The Chronological Table (pp. 37–38) places historical facts alongside biblical and other narratives to help the reader understand their context with the great events that have shaped civilisations.

We must thank the late Kenneth Grant, who inspired us to dig deeper into the mysteries of Thelema than we might otherwise have dared—since the subject has been fenced around with religiose superstition and taboo. I should also mention that our book is in no way a study of the thought or the magical practices of Aleister Crowley. It is in every way an 'unofficial'—and therefore entirely independent—commentary on Liber AL vel Legis. As an instructional work, it is about *how* one may think, not *what* one should think or believe.

Love is the law, love under will.

Oliver St. John

Revised Sol in ♄ 2016 e.v. Anno V–1
St. Ives, Cornwall

The Star of Revealing

In the year 1904 while in Cairo, Egypt, Aleister and Rose Crowley unwittingly earthed the magical transmission or prophetic utterance named Liber AL vel Legis, the Book of the Law. The contents of the book are rooted in the Egyptian Gnostic Tradition. More particularly, the book reveals the Great Work of the Egyptian priests of Ankh-af-na-khonsu, Initiates who vowed to become *Ma-Kheru*—one whose "word is made perfect in Maat". The Great Work of the Initiatic cult of Ankh-af-na-khonsu was the magical transmutation of the soul and the knowledge of the spiritual and natural law governing this operation. The formula of this opus was recorded on the funeral stone of one such Initiate, and is called the *Stele of Revealing*, of which Liber AL vel Legis is a theurgical activation.

Over three chapters, the two hundred and twenty verses of Liber AL vel Legis convey a Hermetic discourse to the Thelemic aspirant. The Egyptian Book of the Law transmits key knowledge concerning the union of the soul with that which lies wholly beyond and outside the human personality. Herein are the mysteries of the soul, veiled as the "Scarlet Woman", and of her transfiguration by the Law of Thelema. The colour of the soul is that of blood and fire. Her nature is lunar and therefore magical and elemental. In union with the solar fire of the transmitter of the will current called the "Beast" she is able to attain Hadit—who conveys the knowledge of her True Will. Through Thelema or love under will she is fully realised as a star in the infinite body of Nuit.

To attain Hadit—the magical manifester of Nuit—the soul must turn her power inwards, turning time backwards on itself. Such is the work of Initiation and the key to self-knowledge. It is only by this inward turning, which often implies a reversal of conventional attitudes and beliefs, that man is afforded full spiritual realisation through union with what is metaphorically termed as the Holy Guardian Angel. Conjoined with the Beast, the Scarlet Woman represents the self-polarisation of the Initiate. Her consciousness is magically directed towards a union of solar fire and lunar magnetism. The child of this union is born of Nuit and Hadit, who communicate through the Beast and the Scarlet Woman, the Prophet and Bride. The divine offspring is Ra Hoor Khuit, Horus the Crowned and Conquering Child of the Gods.

The Threefold Revelation of the Book of the Law

Liber AL vel Legis opens the eye of the soul to the mysteries of immortal life. In so doing, the book brings new meaning and possibilities to the earth life, freeing the soul from all that which confines and enslaves her to sorrow and death. The book speaks of an eternity that rests on relationship: individual existence defining itself by contrast with another by which it can know itself. 'One' can only know itself by comparison with 'minus one', its opposite: that which it is *not*.

The infinite possibilities begotten by relationship are the key of the doorway to eternity. Initiates of Ankh-af-na-khonsu, the Theban priest mentioned in the book, assumed the symbol of the Egyptian ankh or key of life as their magical identity, their name. The book has summarised the spiritual path in seven words: "Love is the law, love under will."

The three chapters of the book each reveal a level of Initiation. From the point of view of practical magick, the book begins with chapter three, not one. Wisdom has to be followed back to her source. The work thus begins in chapter three with Ra Hoor Khuit, the Solar-Hermetic Lucifer whose action upon the soul prepares her for Initiation. His instructions largely concern works of sorcery aimed at overcoming all obstacles encountered on the path. For the soul, such preparations are war. They require an intelligent use of all her resources in order to deal effectively with enemies that are driven by the blind forces of the material universe.

The establishment of Ra Hoor Khuit at the heart or centre of the soul leads to her encounter with Hadit, the giver of Life who speaks through chapter two of the book. The encounter confers upon the Initiate the keys of the knowledge of life that can only be known through the knowledge of death. Through her union with Hadit, the soul contracts; she withdraws from the volatility of sensory perceptions to be stabilised or alchemically 'fixed' as a star in the body of Nuit. Thus, the way is open for the soul to partake of the joys of Nuit, infinitely expanding in her divine ecstasy and love. Chapter one, the voice of Nuit, reveals the secret means of enjoying without restriction the ultimate relationship of opposites: that of individual consciousness and infinity.

I invoke, I greet thy presence, O Ra-Hoor-Khuit!

Liber AL vel Legis, III: 37

Love under Will

To be initiated into the mysteries of Thelema is to be initiated into the mysteries of life, love and death.[6] The meaning of life is love, as proclaimed by Nuit who declares:

For I am divided for love's sake, for the chance of union. This is the creation of the world, that the pain of division is as nothing, and the joy of dissolution all.

Liber AL vel Legis, I: 29–30

The knowledge of life and love comes about through death, the medium of transformation. After such an eclipse has taken place in the dreaming inner landscape of the soul, "that which remains" is the True Will, Thelema.

Remember all ye that existence is pure joy; that all the sorrows are but as shadows; they pass & are done; but there is that which remains.

Liber AL vel Legis, II: 9

The world was created for love by the division of the soul and her spirit. It was created for the chance of their union. Death came into the world so that man could receive the spiritual knowledge of the True Will—the flame of love that burns within his heart, his real identity.

I am the flame that burns in every heart of man, and in the core of every star. I am Life, and the giver of Life, yet therefore is the knowledge of me the knowledge of death.

Liber AL vel Legis, II: 6

---

[6] Thelema, "Will", is written in Greek (Θελημα) in Liber AL vel Legis, I: 39, and may be pronounced "Thelaymah" (classical Greek) or "Theleemah" (modern Greek), with the emphasis on the second syllable in both cases.

The Law of Thelema, love under will, is the means of knowing truth. Liber AL vel Legis instructs the Initiate concerning the nature of this love, which is always returned to Nuit since she is its source. She repeatedly tells the Initiate that all love must be, "To me", "unto me", and "always in the love of me".[7] To fulfil this—the ultimate magical spell—the soul must know who Nuit is. She then understands this wilful aiming of the arrows of love "for the chance of union". Nuit describes herself thus: "I am Infinite Space, and the Infinite Stars thereof" (Liber AL vel Legis, I: 22).[8] And what then, are these stars?

Every man and every woman is a star.

Liber AL vel Legis, I: 3

By Greek Qabalah, Thelema is identical to spiritual love:

Thelema	(Will)	=	93
Agape	(Love)	=	93

We are given to understand that to "love under will" is to love unto Nuit "for the chance of union". That is, to partake of love that brings us to the joy of dissolution. Such love transcends even the spell of death, for it does not bind the soul to those creatures she loves. Instead, she achieves Hadit—the magical manifester of Nuit who gave separate existence for the chance of union.

The lover of Thelema is taken out of himself. His soul is then able to move through creation informed by the 93 current of love under will—which transforms the soul it passes through, giving her substance. To "take your fill and will of love as ye will, when, where and with whom ye will!" is to receive and communicate the 93 current in a love that gathers and returns all to Nuit—"But always unto me" (Liber AL vel Legis, I: 51).

---

[7] See Liber AL vel Legis, I: 51–53, I: 61–63 and I: 65.

[8] The capitalisation reveals that Nuit identifies herself with the goddess ISIS.

Wisdom discerns a difference between the True Will and the personal will. Likewise, between the love of Nuit and the sensory, narcissistic type of love called *Eros* by the ancient Greeks—for the Greeks understood *Eros* to be inseparable from *Thanatos*, death.[9] Hedonism or the satisfaction of *Eros* for its own sake leads to death, for it binds the life force of the natural soul to a body that is corruptible and perishable. *Thanatos*, the dark shadow of *Eros,* refers not only to mortality but also metaphorically to the loss of spiritual life and love. It embodies the idea of the misery of the soul arising from sin, which begins on earth but lasts and increases after the death of the body in hell (or the underworld). In the widest sense it alludes to a tragedy even greater than this.[10]

The purpose of the Great Work is to transform *Eros,* the natural love of the Scarlet Woman or soul, into a vehicle capable of overcoming the power of *Thanatos.* Thelema (93) or love under will is identical to the love called *Agape* (93) by the ancient Greeks. *Agape* is "that which remains" after the death of the physical body, as opposed to *Eros* which—at best—merely vanishes away. What is left of man when he dies, if anything remains at all, is the love that has united him to the love of Nuit, a bond that endures beyond physical death. *Agape* is that love which binds souls together for the purpose of bringing them back to Nuit. Yet such a reward cannot be bargained for; in the final measure it is Nuit herself who chooses her lovers.

When *Agape* or love under will passes through the soul she is transfigured. If *Eros* alone animates her, then she is under the spell of its shadow *Thanatos*. She cuts herself off from the 93 current. As a natural result of the spiritual Law of Thelema she then suffers progressive degradation and loss of substance.

---

[9] *Eros* is here used to refer to sexual and narcissistic love, not to the principle of relatedness in human activities as the psychologist Carl Jung interpreted it. The desirous arrows fired from the bow of *Eros* are inseparable from the idea of fate, and consequently of death. The fated aspect of *Eros* owes to the passivity of will that is the condition of its usual mode of operation.

[10] In Liber AL vel Legis, I: 22, Nuit tells the Initiate: "Bind nothing! Let there be no difference made between any one thing & any other thing; for thereby there cometh hurt." This injunction against "binding" is given as a warning against the natural soul's tendency to bind things to herself, and therefore to finality and multiplicity, the world of "differences" between things. The bond of *Agape*, on the other hand, does not bind things in nature thus causing finite differentiation. It unites them to that which is beyond visible nature.

This need not be understood as a *moral* consequence. No one would attach moral significance to the fact of a rotten apple falling from a tree in a storm. Thelema is a statement of the spiritual facts of life; it does not give a set of arbitrary rules or conditions that are supposed to be 'lived up to'. The natural soul or *prima materia* must therefore be torn apart or dissembled by the wheels set in motion by the 93 current. Dying the "self slain" death of an Initiate she returns that which sprang from the source of Nuit. Only then is she able to break open the shell of her separate existence. The Law of Thelema calls her to silence the empty echo of her own voice so that she may know the beauty of Nuit:

Also for beauty's sake and love's!

Liber AL vel Legis, III: 56

The love and worship of Nuit is to be understood as nocturnal. That is, it does not take place in the ordinary waking conscious mode attributed to the day, but in the fleeting, tenuous and oftentimes elusive shadow realm of night wherein the real and the imagined are no longer contradictory. Yet the conscious (or solar) will is to play a vital part in this, for Nuit is known not only by discerning when, where and with whom to love, but by choosing *how* to love.

Invoke me under my stars! Love is the law, love under will. Nor let the fools mistake love; for there are love and love. There is the dove, and there is the serpent. Choose ye well.

Liber AL vel Legis, I: 57

The choice is to be made wisely. Suppression is no better than self-indulgence. If the soul silences the flesh by an act of violence, the flesh will take revenge upon the soul, secretly infecting her with a spirit of revenge. It is an error to suppose that spiritual life is a mere negation of matter. By the magick of Thelema everything we have to offer—mind body and soul—is to serve the Great Work through its intimate relation with the 93 current of love under will. In this way, the principle of life itself is sought above and beyond the deceptive human nature. Hadit the giver of Life lives in the world loving all things equally, yet in perfect freedom.

Hadit reminds us: "Be not animal; refine thy rapture!" (Liber AL vel Legis, II: 70.) He invites the soul to fully experience all the joys of incarnation, calling forth man's lust as a means of knowing the joys that inebriate the soul:

I am the Snake that giveth Knowledge & Delight and bright glory, and stir the hearts of men with drunkenness. To worship me take wine and strange drugs whereof I will tell my prophet, & be drunk thereof! They shall not harm ye at all. It is a lie, this folly against self. The exposure of innocence is a lie. Be strong, o man! lust, enjoy all things of sense and rapture: fear not that any God shall deny thee for this.

Liber AL vel Legis, II: 22

This drunkenness is Nuit herself, who urges her lovers thus:

I love you! I yearn to you! Pale or purple, veiled or voluptuous, I who am all pleasure and purple, and drunkenness of the innermost sense, desire you. Put on the wings, and arouse the coiled splendour within you: come unto me!

Liber AL vel Legis, I: 61

The Thelemite desires and thirsts for an ecstasy that frees the soul while transmuting her substance. The wine that so inebriates the soul is the 93 current of love under will.

The Hermetic Great Work

Obey my prophet! follow out the ordeals of my knowledge! seek me only! Then the joys of my love will redeem ye from all pain. This is so: I swear it by the vault of my body; by my sacred heart and tongue; by all I can give, by all I desire of ye all.

Liber AL vel Legis, I: 32

With the passing of time the face of eternity takes on new expressions in human consciousness. As the World Soul passes through her cyclical changes, so the divine Word or Logos modifies his utterance to preserve creation from inertia. Nothing in the universe remains static; likewise, the relationship between God and man has its phases of development.

The primary rule of spiritual law is universal as expressed through the worldwide mystical and religious practices of the last two millennia: to be redeemed from suffering and death, man must sacrifice his personal will to that of God. Yet through the ages, what is revealed to mankind about the mysteries of the life of his soul undergoes transformation.

Liber AL vel Legis or the Egyptian Book of the Law proclaims the spiritual law of the present age. Death is overcome by fixing the volatile, that is, by the transfiguration of the mutable elements of the natural soul.

The present age is a nuclear age, and so Liber AL vel Legis reveals the atomic nature of man and God. By means of a nuclear reaction taking place at the spiritual level the transfiguration of the human soul is accomplished. The book addresses a prophet, the Theban high priest Ankh-af-na-khonsu—whose name was adopted by all members of an Initiatic cult. Aleister Crowley believed that his mission was the magical communication of this knowledge to the men and women of his time. Liber AL vel Legis calls this knowledge Thelema, the True Will.

For those called to follow the path of Initiation, God is to be understood as both *nothing* and *two*. As nothing, God is the unfathomable depth beyond creation; as two, God is the androgynous binary intelligence begetting infinite possibilities of existence. These in turn preserve the equilibrium of the universe. The dual aspects of the eternal are named after the most abstract Egyptian gods, Nuit and Hadit.

Nuit and Hadit are identical to the Mother and Son of the ancient Typhonian mysteries that predate the notion of God as "Father".[11] Nuit is the goddess of infinite space while Hadit is her manifester—her Word and her Will. He is the infinite contraction that begets individual consciousness. The body of Nuit is "heaven", in which each individual centre of consciousness is a star:

The unveiling of the company of heaven.
Every man and every woman is a star.

Liber AL vel Legis, I: 2–3

The Intelligence revealed by the two hundred and twenty verses of Liber AL vel Legis is a begetter of change and multiplicity who assumes many names. Each refers to a particular phase of the life cycle of creation. The origin and destination of the life cycle know one another intimately, and the space between them is created for the bliss of its transcendence.

For I am divided for love's sake, for the chance of union.
This is the creation of the world, that the pain of division is as nothing, and the joy of dissolution all.

Liber AL vel Legis, I: 29–30

The manifold names of the Intelligence revealed in Liber AL vel Legis should not lead us to assume that a regression is implied. Instead, man is called to knowledge that transcends the limitations of monotheism. Polytheism, correctly understood, allows for the fullest expression of the divine in nature whereas monotheism leads to a dualistic impasse, dissociating from its religious idea of God all those things that threaten human ideals and conventions.[12]

---

[11] Typhon is the Greek name for the multi-faceted god who perpetually brings about change in the universe. He appears in mythology under many names, including: Hadit, Set, Bes, or "the Beast". One of his symbols is the Egyptian Sphinx. He is the son who manifests his mother, the primal goddess, taking on any number of forms and aspects. In a certain sense, all pre-religious cults that emphasise a feminine Creatrix are "Typhonian".

[12] Both E. A. Wallis Budge and R. A. Schwaller de Lubicz have suggested that ancient Egyptian polytheism was *not* a fragmented view of creation, as has been put forward by monotheist theologians.

Thelema, however, is infinitely subtle. The Creator (or Creatrix) is *polymorphous*. The forms apprehended by consciousness conceal the Hidden One who is really none, or two.[13] Manifested existence is a perennial process of self-renewal, and the universe finds stability through change—through the constant making and breaking of identities. Like the *ouroboros*, the great serpent that eats its own tail, and the pelican that feeds its children on its own blood, life periodically consumes itself to be recreated.

This shall regenerate the world, the little world my sister, my heart & my tongue, unto whom I send this kiss.

Liber AL vel Legis, I: 53

Thelema calls the Initiate to understand a primary duality: the infinity of Nuit, who is manifested by Hadit, her Word, her sacred heart or star. To be informed by Hadit, the soul or Scarlet Woman must receive the communication from Horus or Ra Hoor Khuit. By the power of his magick Hadit sends forth Horus, and the result is a polarisation of consciousness:

Now let it be first understood that I am a god of War and Vengeance. I shall deal hardly with them.

Liber AL vel Legis, III: 3

Liber AL vel Legis is the book of the Last Judgement, the ultimate initiatory trial and nuclear transformation passed through by the soul.[14] Thelema is a weighing of the heart and a considerable spiritual ordeal.

---

[13] The "Hidden One" is a name of the Egyptian god Amoun. He is referred to as "Amen" in Liber AL vel Legis, II: 49.

[14] The letter "L" which appears in the title of the book, Liber AL vel Legis, corresponds Qabalistically to the Hebrew letter Lamed. In the Tarot, this letter corresponds to Atu VIII, *Adjustment*, attributed to the astrological sign of Libra, the Scales of the Egyptian goddess Maat. Maat is the ruler and preserver of universal equilibrium; she is an embodiment of the principle, both natural and cosmic, of justice, that is, justification. Justification, as the title of Crowley's Tarot trump suggests, is ongoing and continuous.

Such ordeals may be subtle and not even realised by the aspirant. The ambiguous nature of the Thelemic source text lends itself easily to the idiocy of fundamentalist interpretation. It is a book to listen to with the heart; reason alone is fated to suffer its curses. The book declares that, "the exposure of innocence is a lie" (Liber AL vel Legis, II: 22); its effect is to strip the soul naked before the unrelenting eye of Horus, the Avenging Angel.

The Last Judgement operates on three levels. Firstly, it makes possible the magical and mystical Initiation of the incarnated soul. This prepares her for the second level, the spiritual overcoming of physical death. Both of these levels are individual. The third level is universal since it operates through a collective adjustment that takes place at the end of each great age or aeon.

Aeons may be perceived as either objective and historic, or subjective and dwelling beyond or outside of time. An historic aeon results from the objectification of a subjective aeon; that is, the passing into time of a deeper stratum of consciousness that is pre-existent.

The Last Judgement presents itself at the end of a period of time, or at the apotheosis of a type of consciousness. The end of time and the full bloom of consciousness may be coincidental, but they are never completely merged as no period of time manifests a single, unique level of consciousness. Individuals functioning in different modes of Aeonic consciousness or spiritual awareness have cohabited on earth throughout the ages, even though the collective consciousness of each age has a dominant character. This may at times give rise to fierce battles, spiritual or otherwise. The Thelemite must be well prepared for such encounters.

The Law of Thelema places the individual in a face-to-face confrontation with all the potentiality for good and evil within the soul. It is therefore "the law of the strong" (Liber AL vel Legis, II: 21). The 'church' uniting the disciples of Thelema is a magical body that is formed by their hearts and souls. Whilst the 93 current threatens to destroy all that is inimical to it, the Great Work of returning the soul to the love and joy of Nuit is nonetheless its primary aim. Thelema brings a new dimension to the relationship between the human and the divine. A magical pathway to the stars is offered to those capable of navigating it— and who are prepared for the consequences of receiving forbidden knowledge. "Forbidden", because it refutes the doctrines of the scriptural and other laws that are superimposed upon the direct experience now considered to be occult. Yet the Law of Thelema is at the same time a universal one—universal because it is so particular:

Do what thou wilt shall be the whole of the Law.

Liber AL vel Legis, I: 40

An Initiate is therefore wholly responsible for the particular expression of the True Will in his own existence. This implies a most intimate, direct and conscious relationship with Hadit, the Word that informs him. Thelema aims at bringing man to a new level of consciousness and spiritual maturity. To achieve this, the Initiate must transcend the ideologies that produce the evils of self-righteousness, intolerance, and tyrannical repression. As Nuit so concisely whispers to her followers:

The word of Sin is Restriction.

Liber AL vel Legis, I: 41

Thelema confers knowledge that puts earthly existence in a new perspective. To know the infinite is to pass beyond the suffering and sorrow that inevitably result from identification with the finite.

Remember all ye that existence is pure joy; that all the sorrows are but as shadows; they pass & are done; but there is that which remains.

Liber AL vel Legis, II: 9

The Sphinx: Symbol of the Polymorphous God

The Law of Thelema is intimately related to the mysteries of a God who, being both none and two, creates the world through parthenogenesis. As two, the divine androgyne is the source of infinite combinations and possibilities of existence. Androgyny and polymorphism go hand in hand. As two, the divine androgyne has the power to form atomic nuclei of consciousness and give them many forms by inducing reactions and bonds between them. Each and every moment of awareness in space-time is an atom of consciousness manifested by the androgyne as either 'self' or 'other'.

Hidden at the heart of creation, the enigmatic Word is a shape-shifter. He and the world he creates around him take on new forms over time, and the pattern of their transformation is marked by periodicity. They do not move in a straight line but as a curve that comes back on itself time and time again, regenerated by the cyclical shedding of its skin. From Liber AL vel Legis emerges a law of relativity; although Nuit is eternal and constant, her Will in creation depends upon time and place. Nothing in creation is of universal and absolute application. Nonetheless, some things are truly ordained whilst others miss the mark, being out of time and out of place, or without love. The Law of Thelema is particular in that it is time-sensitive.

The begetter of change takes on many names, each a word or form displayed to the soul to help her understand her true nature. Thus she is able to consciously participate in the universal life cycle while remaining united to Hadit who springs from and returns to eternity. The means of so doing is referred to in Liber AL vel Legis as the Beast, who was known to the Egyptians as Hu, the Sphinx. Liber AL vel Legis uses the Greek variant of this name: Hrumachis.[15] The many forms assumed by the Beast in the book each have their name, such as Ra, Heru-ra-ha, Ra Hoor Khuit, Hoor-paar-kraat, Tum, Khephra and Ahathoor (Hathoor). These gods are all expressions of the atomic, solar, conscious and transformative power of Mind hidden in creation yet animating it.

---

[15] "Harmachis" is the conventional spelling—see E. A. Wallis Budge, *The Gods of the Egyptians.*

13

The Egyptian Sphinx is the most ancient symbol of the androgynous and polymorphous god to be found on earth today. The Beast or the Sphinx Hrumachis is an aspect of Horus, the Crowned and Conquering Child of the Gods who, like the sun, perpetually arises renewed from his journey through the cycle of creation. Hrumachis is closely related to the ancient god Bes, who is probably of either Semitic or African origin and represented by a dwarf. Bes, "the aged one who makes himself young again", was worshipped in early Egyptian dynasties; by the time of the New Kingdom he became identified with Horus the child, Hoor paar kraat. Little by little, Bes was merged with other forms of the sun god such as Horus, Ra and Tum until at length he absorbed their qualities. As such, Bes moved into a close relationship with Hrumachis. By the XXVIth dynasty (663 to 525 BCE) Bes was merged completely in Horus, with whom he shared the attribute of Lord of all the Typhonian Beasts.

With a lion's body and a human face, the Sphinx represents the dual nature of creation and the interaction of matter and spirit, of the bestial and the human. The lion and the woman are symbols of the astrological signs of Leo and Aquarius, the "Star & the Snake" of Liber AL vel Legis.[16] The Star and Snake are Nuit and Hadit, dual aspects of the androgynous god who, as two, is a polymorphous creator. Of Hrumachis, there will be more to tell, for the wheel of the aeons turned at the dawning of the 21st century. Hrumachis has arisen at the "fall of the Great Equinox":[17]

But your holy place shall be untouched throughout the centuries: though with fire and sword it be burnt down & shattered, yet an invisible house there standeth, and shall stand until the fall of the Great Equinox; when Hrumachis shall arise and the double-wanded one assume my throne and place.

Liber AL vel Legis, III: 34

---

[16] "The Sun, Strength & Sight, Light; these are for the servants of the Star & the Snake" (Liber AL vel Legis, II: 21).

[17] By the tropical (or solar) Zodiac the Sun always enters the sign of Aries at the spring equinox, and that of Libra at the autumn equinox. However by the sidereal (or stellar) Zodiac, the Sun now enters the sign of Aquarius at the spring equinox and Leo at the autumn equinox. This is the "fall of the Great Equinox", for the precessional Great Year of 26,000 years begins at Leo the Lion, according to the wisdom of the ancient Egyptians. We are now at the exact mid point of the wheel of time—the "fall" or autumn of the Great Year.

The Atomic Transfiguration of the Beast 666

The Beast or Sphinx is a symbol of life. Physical life is manifested by the creation and animation of matter, of which the smallest component is the atom. Man and the atom are closely related: the atom acts as the building block of matter in the universe; the fulfilment of man is to act as the building block of consciousness.

The development of matter and consciousness follow an identical pattern. This is very well symbolised by the numerical progression that forms the Qabalistic Tree of Life. Atoms assemble to form chemical elements that in turn combine to create molecules. Likewise, human beings communicate so as to form increasingly universal levels of knowledge and understanding.

An atom consists of a positively charged nucleus surrounded by a cloud of negatively charged electrons. In most atoms the nucleus is dual, composed of two types of particles: positively charged protons, and neutrally charged neutrons. The nucleus of the atom is analogous to the nucleus formed by man and his spiritual counterpart, the Holy Guardian Angel or *Khabs* ("star"). The Angel is a positive charge like the proton; man is a neutral charge that is magnetically directed, like the neutron. The electron cloud surrounding the atom is as the body of Nuit or *Khu*, of which each electron is "everywhere the centre" like Hadit:

In the sphere I am everywhere the centre, as she, the circumference, is nowhere found.

Liber AL vel Legis, II: 3

Electrons cannot be split into anything smaller; they do not have any real size but are instead true points in space—for an electron has a radius of zero, like Hadit who is "not extended":

Come! all ye, and learn the secret that hath not yet been revealed. I, Hadit, am the complement of Nu, my bride. I am not extended, and Khabs is the name of my House.

Liber AL vel Legis, II: 2

15

The simplest element is hydrogen. Its atoms are the smallest as they only contain one proton and one electron. The nucleus of a hydrogen atom contains no neutron. Pure hydrogen exists as hydrogen gas in which pairs of hydrogen atoms bond together to make larger particles called molecules. When hydrogen gas burns in air it forms water, hence its name that derives from the Greek words for "water former". On the Tree of Life of Qabalah, hydrogen corresponds to the sphere of Chokmah and the archetypal world Atziluth. Hydrogen atoms were among the first atoms to form in the early universe.

According to the "big bang" theory, hydrogen nuclei—protons—formed within three minutes after the unimaginable explosion that scientists believe to have created the universe. The protons began to combine with electrons to form hydrogen atoms when the universe was about 300,000 years old. The process of combination continued until the universe was about one million years old. In stars, hydrogen nuclei combine with each other in nuclear reactions to build helium atoms that contain two electrons, two protons and two neutrons. Helium is the first element containing neutrons in its nucleus. These high-energy reactions create the light and heat of the Sun and most other stars. On the Tree of Life, helium corresponds to the sephira of Binah and the creative world Briah.

Virtually all atoms are made in the interior of stars during a supernova—the explosion of a star that emits vast amounts of energy. The explosions build atoms in thermonuclear reactions—high temperature events that fuse two nuclei together. Hydrogen atoms fuse together into a helium atom and then helium atoms fuse into carbon whose atomic number is 6. Carbon atoms can then fuse with helium into oxygen whose atomic number is 8.[18]

Carbon corresponds to the sphere of Tiphereth and oxygen to Da'ath—which is the eighth (or hidden) sephira of the Tree if we count upwards from Malkuth.

---

[18] Placing the elements on the Hermetic Tree of Life, we have: hydrogen corresponding to Chokmah, helium corresponding to Binah, and carbon to Tiphereth. Placing the atomic particles on the Hermetic Tree, we have Kether corresponding to the electron, Chokmah to the proton, and Binah to the neutron. The correspondences between the Four Worlds of the Qabalah and the atom are: the electron, Atziluth; the electron cloud, Briah; the proton, Yetzirah; the neutron, Assiah. See "The Master Key to Atomic Thelemic Correspondences" in the Appendices.

Oxygen may also be compared with the Ruach, extending the latter to the eight sephiroth from Binah to Malkuth. Oxygen may then form molecules with hydrogen to produce water, the matrix of life. The fundamental building block of material in living organisms is the carbon atom that is composed of 6 electrons, 6 protons and 6 neutrons.[19] The three sixes form the number 666, the number of the Beast mentioned in the Revelation of St. John, 13: 18:

"Here is wisdom. Let him that hath understanding count the number of the beast: for it is the number of a man; and his number is Six hundred threescore and six."

Revelation tells us that 666 is the number of the Beast and the number of a man. In so doing, the final book of the Bible gives an everlasting symbol of the relationship between man and the universe. The symbol rests on the analogy mentioned above: carbon, the building block of organic matter; and man, the building block of universal consciousness. The most ancient representation of the Beast to be found on earth today is the Egyptian Sphinx who stands on the plateau of Giza next to the pyramids. The physical basis of the pyramid as a symbol is carbon, or carbon as a diamond crystal. Diamond is the hardest natural material known, owing to the particular arrangement of its crystalline structure. The structure consists of interlinking tetrahedrons of carbon forming an infinite matrix of covalent bonds. A tetrahedron is a solid having four plane triangular faces. Thus, on the plateau of Giza lies the image of the supranatural destiny of man, by which his subtle structure is transfigured by being fixed in an indestructible configuration that leans both inside and outside of time.

The metaphysical law of transfiguration is the law of love under will, whose core message is clear: the transmutation of the spiritual structure of man takes place through the seamless merging of his personal will, which is his earthly vehicle or transmitter, and the True Will. The Word of the True Will is a force flowing through the universe as a magnetic current capable of reorganising and spiritualising the elements of creation.

---

[19] Six is the number of Tiphereth, attributed to the Sun, while 666 is the Qabalistic number of its Kamea or magic square. The numbers six hundred, sixty, and six are the equivalent, by Qabalistic Aiq Bekir, of the spiritual phallus ("image), Vav, the letter and path of *The Hierophant V* of Tarot.

The carbon analogy provides a useful basis for understanding the Great Work of alchemy and magick. When combining with itself, carbon forms two substances: graphite and diamond. Graphite is very soft and slippery whereas diamond is the hardest, most stable substance known. The different properties come about through the manner in which carbon atoms form bonds with each other. In graphite, the carbon atoms are arranged in layers; only weak forces exist between layers. This allows layers of carbon to slide over each other. In other words, the body produced by these bonds is mutable, not fixed—the condition of the instinctive soul of nature or Qabalistic Nephesch. On the other hand, in diamond the carbon atoms are equidistant and form a rigid, immovable network. The volatile has been fixed into a star capable of receiving and transmitting extremely subtle impressions. Alchemical language describes this as the Immortal Stone. In like manner, the fabric of the natural soul may be transformed. Her elements are irradiated and organised by the True Will or 93 current so as to allow the ingress and egress of cosmic intelligence. This occurs via the infinite matrix or celestial body of Nuit, which is the channel or recipient for the "pure river of water of life, clear as a crystal, proceeding out of the throne of God and of the Lamb" shown by the angel to St. John in the book of Revelation 22: 1. The soul arising triumphant from death is described in Revelation as the crystalline heavenly Jerusalem:

"Come hither, I will shew thee the bride, the Lamb's wife. And he carried me away in the spirit to a great and high mountain, and shewed me that great city, the holy Jerusalem, descending out of heaven from God, having the glory of God: and her light was like unto a stone most precious, even like a jasper stone, clear as crystal; and had a wall great and high, and had twelve gates, and at the gates twelve angels, and names written thereon, which are the names of the twelve tribes of the children of Israel: On the east three gates; on the north three gates; on the south three gates; and on the west three gates. And the wall of the city had twelve foundations, and in them the names of the twelve apostles of the Lamb. And he that talked with me had a golden reed to measure the city, and the gates thereof, and the wall thereof. And the city lieth foursquare, and the length is as large as the breadth: and he measured the city with the reed, twelve thousand furlongs. The length and the breadth and the height of it are equal. And he measured the wall thereof, an hundred and forty and four cubits, according to the measure of a man, that is, of the angel." (Revelation, 21: 9–17)

The "Lamb" refers to the astrological sign of the Ram, Aries, which the Sun enters at the spring equinox. It is the blood or energy of consecration in magick. The twelve gates of the heavenly Jerusalem can be viewed in the present context as the twelve sides of the diamond tetrahedral structure. These are arranged as four planes or triangular faces, the four directions having three gates each. In this lies a further analogy to the carbon atom, whose outermost electron shell consists of 4 electrons.[20] The shell, also termed "valence shell", can accommodate a total of eight electrons. Carbon requires four more electrons to stabilise its outer shell, and can thus be said to have four openings or "gates" for the formation of bonds.[21] Like the carbon atom, man whose number is 666 has a valence of four: four openings through which to unite with his Holy Guardian Angel. This is the traditional quaternity, cross or crossing which confers Initiation. Hence the words spoken by Hadit in the penultimate verse of Liber AL vel Legis, II: 78:

Lift up thyself! for there is none like unto thee among men or among Gods! Lift up thyself, o my prophet, thy stature shall surpass the stars. They shall worship thy name, foursquare, mystic, wonderful, the number of the man; and the name of thy house 418.

The name of man is foursquare and mystic when he attains the mystical union that is the ultimate goal of magick and yoga. Continuing to use the analogy, his "four" is completed as "eight". The four openings through which a bond may be formed between the human and the cosmic are described thus:

There are four gates to one palace; the floor of that palace is of silver and gold...

Liber AL vel Legis, I: 51

---

[20] Carbon has a total of 6 electrons, 2 orbiting around an innermost shell and 4 orbiting around an outermost or valence shell. To be complete, the carbon valence shell requires 8 electrons. See the Appendices, "The Master Key of Thelemic Atomic Correspondences".
[21] Four is the number of the Hebrew letter Daleth, meaning, "door". On the Hermetic Tree of Life this letter is attributed to the path of Venus (*The Empress*, Tarot Atu III). Venus is love, the doorway to heaven; her symbol is the Ankh of Life representing the union between the human (the cross, duality) and the divine (the circle, infinity).

The palace or "house 418" is the celestial *Khu* or body of Nuit, the heavenly Jerusalem. Its floor of silver and gold bears an analogy to the nucleus of the atom, whose protons radiate a positive charge symbolised by the solar power or gold, and whose neutrons are inert and ghostly as the moon symbolised by silver.

The length and the breadth of the heavenly Jerusalem are of equal measure, that is, the soul and her Holy Guardian Angel become of equal measure. This measure is twelve, the number of the circle of the Zodiac representing the full cycle of creation. Man has become one with the Angel, and the resultant synergy results in a substance that is greater than the sum of its parts. The two "twelves" multiplying each other are now as "an hundred and forty and four". The circle has been squared through Initiation, thus fulfilling the Law of Thelema. The orientation of the four elements of the natural soul to the four gates of the cosmic has been brought to perfection. Thus the intelligence that is the love of Nuit may flow between them forever and forever. Added together, 666 and 144 yield 810, the number of the Chaldean word ShMINITh.[22] The word ShMINITh means "octave", a series of eight notes occupying the interval between (and including) two musical notes, one having twice or half the frequency of vibration of the other. The musical octave may symbolise the full range of consciousness from unknowing darkness to luminous knowledge, from the isolated carbon atom to the diamond matrix of infinity. This loop of infinity is the very substance of the polymorphic god who proclaims that he is "eight, and one in eight":

With the just I am eight, and one in eight: Which is vital, for I am none indeed.

Liber AL vel Legis, II: 15

The polymorphic god acts upon creation as the invisible electron cloud or quantum field magnetises the atom nucleus. The cloud is a womb for the formation of the curvature of time and space; through this continuum travels Hadit, the magical Word and Will of Nuit. Hadit flows as an energy current intelligently ordering the cosmos through his communication with creation. Compare with Genesis, 9: 16:

---

[22] By Gematria, or Qabalistic correspondence.

"And the bow shall be in the cloud; and I will look upon it, that I may remember the everlasting covenant between God and every living creature of all flesh that is upon the earth."

The electron is the physical manifestation of the magnetic "rod of iron" with which the Word comes to "smite the nations" in the book of Revelation, 19: 15:

"And out of his mouth goeth a sharp sword, that with it he should smite the nations: and he shall rule them with a rod of iron: and he treadeth the winepress of the fierceness and wrath of Almighty God."

In the nucleus of the cosmic atom dwells the dual building block of consciousness: man, whose ultimate destiny is the union that results in being born as a star in the heaven of Nuit.

The Beast and Leviathan

The idea of a universe made of unbalanced forces seeking completion through bonding with other unbalanced forces lies at the basis of the Qabalistic doctrine of the Qliphoth or "shells". The shells, which by analogy with atomic theory are as the valence shell of the atom, are drawn together by their tendency to seek stability through mutual exchanges of energy. Assembled by atomic bonding, the Qliphoth form the body of the great dragon called Leviathan in the Old Testament. The body of Leviathan is mutable and polymorphic; the units forming it are forever decaying while their dispersed elements are recycled to assemble as new forms.

The body of Leviathan is an image not only of the mutability of the physical universe but also of human souls who, incomplete by nature, seek stability through union with other unbalanced forces. The purpose of the Great Work is to transmute by the power of magick the Qliphoth or unbalanced forces of the universe from their incompleteness by uniting them to that which is fixed or constant as opposed to that which is transient and perishable. "Love under will", on the other hand, is a magical art of universal application. The love or bonding capacity of the unbalanced forces is not merely suppressed in the hope of attaining something better, but is directed by the 93 current or True Will towards Nuit consciousness.

The doctrine of the Qliphoth is identical to that of the transmutation of the Beast 666 and, to refer to the analogy of atomic theory, the stabilisation of the carbon atom as diamond. The most useful exposition of this doctrine is given in a text entitled, *The Book of Concealed Mystery*.[23] Its elements are as follows:

1. Shells, excavations or receptacles have fallen into the world of creation. These form a Great Dragon that is in the sea, and is "not so harmful as the earthly one". These shells are subject to judgement.

---

[23] *The Book of Concealed Mystery* by Knorr Van Rosenroth was translated by MacGregor Mathers and published under the title, *Kabbalah Unveiled*.

This describes the formation of matter, the basic component of which is the atom. The structure of the atom is "the secret that hath not yet been revealed" (Liber AL vel Legis, II: 2).[24] Leviathan is a large fire-breathing animal. Just as the bombardier beetle has an explosion producing mechanism—it discharges an irritant vapour from its anus with an audible pop when alarmed—so the great sea dragon has an explosion producing mechanism to enable it to be a "fire breathing dragon." Continuing with the atom analogy, this dragon is a symbol of "big bang", and of supernovas. The name "Leviathan" comes from the Chaldean word LVH, meaning, "to join, lend, borrow". Leviathan therefore represents an explosion, producing units of consciousness (or atoms) that are joined by the lending and borrowing of energy (or electrons) to form the universe.

The Qliphoth or shells represent that which is incomplete and born of division—as does man as the fallen Beast 666 or the carbon atom. The shells may be compared to the valence layer or shell of the atom—"excavations" or "receptacles" containing openings in which to receive energy (electrons) from other units. The "judgement" to which the Qliphoth are subject is the law of equilibration, called the Law of Maat by the ancient Egyptians.[25] The Avenging Angel Ra Hoor Khuit is the enforcer of the Law of Maat, causing change and movement so that balance or equilibration may be found through union with other atoms. Unstable units are destroyed; their components disperse to be rearranged in other life forms. The doctrine of the Qliphoth states that the sea dragon is not as harmful as the earthly one, for earthly bonds most effectively cancel out the possibility of spiritual discipline. In the Initiated traditions the doctrine of the Qliphoth applies to the use of the Leviathan force within the individual.

---

[24] The verse number 2: 2 is indicative of the relationship between atomic theory and the twenty-two scales of the serpent or dragon, Leviathan.

[25] Maat is the Egyptian goddess of justice and balance who watches over the equilibrium of the universe. Her symbols are the feather of truth and the scales, and she is attributed to the astrological sign of Libra. On the Tree of Life, Libra corresponds to path 22, Lamed, and Atu VIII, *Adjustment*. Lamed is the Hebrew letter "L" from which Liber AL vel Legis derives its title. Liber AL vel Legis is therefore the Book of the Law of Maat, the law of justification and of the Last Judgement. The number 8 of Maat's Tarot trump is the number of the completion of the carbon atom's valence shell.

23

Through magical practice, Leviathan manifests as the *Kundalini* or Occult Force. It is the power of Hadit, symbolised by the Serpent in Liber AL vel Legis, who warns the Initiate:

I am the secret Serpent coiled about to spring: in my coiling there is joy. If I lift up my head, I and my Nuit are one. If I droop down mine head, and shoot forth venom, then is rapture of the earth, and I and the earth are one.
There is a great danger in me; for who doth not understand these runes shall make a great miss. He shall fall down into the pit called Because, and there he shall perish with the dogs of Reason.

Liber AL vel Legis, II: 26–27

The soul whose desire to bond for completion is not informed by the True Will but is mislead by her reason or controlling ego, perishes in the abyss, the "pit called Because".

2. The dragon has been castrated—crest and mate repressed, and thence have been formed four hundred desirable worlds.

The castration of the dragon represents its incompleteness; it is not self-polarised and has thus lost both crest and mate and is forgetful of the Word. It cannot find completion in itself and is driven forward in an attempt to find stability and equilibration by joining other forces. The "four hundred desirable worlds" are an image of the valence of the carbon atom, the basis of organic life. It desires union with four additional electrons to be completed; in the process it forms 400 worlds. To avoid becoming subject to an unrestrained vampirical force the soul must obtain union with the crossing afforded by the amulet of the fourfold power of Daleth, the Ankh of Life.

3. In the head of the dragon is a nostril through which he receives influence, and this dragon contains all the other dragons.

The influence received by the dragon is Hadit or the Word—shaping its movement in creation and directing the formation of matter under the law of Maat.[26]

---

[26] The ancient Egyptians attributed the Word or Logos to the god Thoth. They regarded him as the god of magick and writing, and the male counterpart of Maat.

24

The dragon and Hadit act to preserve universal equilibrium, destroying that which is unstable and rearranging the parts to form new units of existence. The "influence" is the transmission called the 93 current of Thelema. Its ultimate aim is to stabilise or 'fix the volatile' of the dragon so that spiritual intelligence may emerge through the time tunnel or matrix thus created.

4. His tail is in his head; he is centripetal, not centrifugal, but his head is broken by the waters of the great sea.

The dragon with his tail in his head is the *ouroboros*, a symbol of Saturn. The Greeks knew Saturn as Chronos, a name that means "time"; the legend of this god is that he ate his own children. The *ouroboros* is an image of the perpetual process of creation, destruction, dispersion and assimilation of forms that animates the universe. The purpose of the Great Work is to rescue the soul from this fate; that is, to free her from the lending and borrowing forces that would bind her to the unbalanced shells that, subjected to time, are perpetually devoured by Saturn. To pass beyond time is to "achieve Hadit":

Behold! the rituals of the old time are black. Let the evil ones be cast away; let the good ones be purged by the prophet! Then shall this Knowledge go aright.

Liber AL vel Legis, II: 5

To know Hadit and free herself from the coils of the great dragon the soul must overcome the pull of Saturn. Saturn is the ruler of the physical universe, and rituals that bind the soul to that universe are "black", for they lead her to death.[27] All rituals must therefore be unto Nuit, whose infinite body is not subject to the mutable forces of nature:

If the ritual be not ever unto me: then expect the direful judgments of Ra Hoor Khuit!

Liber AL vel Legis, I: 52

---

[27] The number of the letter of Saturn, Tav, is 400.

The liberation of the soul from sin and death comes about through mastery of the power of the dragon. The soul must overcome the dualism of the material universe, and achieves this through her Initiation into the mysteries of self-polarisation. This involves the magical use of the life force that is embodied in the dragon, her physical body and ego consciousness. The soul may then say with Ra Hoor Khuit:

I am the Lord of the Double Wand of Power; the wand of the Force of Coph Nia—but my left hand is empty, for I have crushed an Universe; & nought remains.

Liber AL vel Legis, III: 72

Being centripetal, the force of the dragon moves towards a centre. The centre is the nucleus of the atom; it is for the purpose of stabilising the nucleus that the dragon seeks to unite with complementary forces. The only true fulfilment of the centripetal force, however, is the union with that which is eternally beyond, and so outside of time. When the centre or nucleus thus attains immortality the shell is likewise perfected. The head of the dragon is broken upon the waters of the great sea, for above the Abyss in the great sea of *Binah*—which also happens to be the body of Nuit—the centrifugal force no longer exists. The motion of the dragon stops; the volatile has been fixed. This is illustrated by the correspondence between *Binah* and the helium atom: helium is a noble gas, complete in itself. Its valence is zero—it binds nothing.

5. He is double and has many heads, embodying the idea of multiplicity; he is the king of all the shells or demons.

Leviathan is "double" in that he has within himself the capacity to lend forces (electrons) to others as well as to borrow from them. He is the king of all shells for he is the archetype of the centripetal force moving towards the fixation of a centre. So long as Leviathan seeks to fix the centre by uniting with other incomplete forces he remains as an unbalanced shell. When united with the eternity outside of time he is no longer demonic; the Qliphoth undergo transmutation, in other words they are no longer subject to death and destruction.

The Sphinx, Time and Alchemy[28]

The Sphinx is an astronomical clock. Its position on the plateau of Giza is precisely aligned with the point on the horizon where the sun rises at the spring equinox. This point is used as a reference to calculate the astronomical cycle known as the precession of the equinoxes—the name given to the progression of the spring or vernal equinoctial point through the twelve constellations of the Zodiac. The full cycle or "Great Year" extends approximately over 26,000 years and comprises twelve astrological ages a little more than 2000 years each.

The mystery of the Sphinx that we are concerned with here is that of the transformation of consciousness over the course of this cycle. It is a cycle that can be seen as both historical and archetypal. The Sphinx is a symbol of the magical manifestations of Hadit, the life-giving spirit. The great clock that surrounds it typifies the mutable, cyclical nature of the life of the universe and of the human soul. The cycle passes through four stages:

1. Creation in eternity
2. The Fall or creation in the world of matter, time and space
3. Death and dissolution of material existence, the "end of time"
4. The return to eternity

The quaternary cycle emerges from out of the doubling or parthenogenesis of the primal polarity manifesting Nuit and Hadit in time and space. The manifestation of Nuit is referred to in Liber AL vel Legis as the "Scarlet Woman"; the manifestation of Hadit is referred to as the "Beast". The manifestation of Nuit is imaged forth by the Zodiac and that of Hadit, by the Sphinx.

The universe, both unmanifest and manifested, thus comprises four cardinal points. Two of them are in eternity, and therefore *outside* of time, and two of them are *in time*. The cardinal points representing eternity are the North and South, Aquarius and Leo, Nuit and Hadit. Together they form the vertical axis of the cross that is the symbol of the universe.

The cardinal points representing time are the East and West, corresponding to the astrological signs of Taurus and Scorpio that in turn represent the Beast and the Scarlet Woman. They stand at each end of the horizon and form the horizontal axis of the cross.

---

[28] See the diagram, "The Sphinx: Life Cycle of Consciousness" (pp. 32).

In classical mythology, the Sphinx is sometimes represented as a fourfold creature bearing the attributes of all four cardinal points. With a human face, the body of a bull, the feet of a lion and the wings of an eagle, the form developed from the original image of the dual Egyptian Sphinx. The name "Sphinx" is derived from the Greek *sphingein* meaning "to draw tight". Creation is a contraction of infinity. *Sphingein* is also the root of the word "sphincter", pointing to the relationship between the symbol of the Sphinx and the aperture through which eternity flows into time. Thus, the divine Word is uttered to beget creation. This aperture is the metaphysical point through which the doubles of Nuit and Hadit—the Scarlet Woman or World Soul and the Beast or World Axis—fall into time and space.

The Zodiac with its four cardinal points is one of the images of the metamorphic life cycle whose mysteries are revealed in Liber AL vel Legis. The Sphinx stands at the heart of its twelve signs, of which four are fixed: Leo, Aquarius, Taurus and Scorpio. These are the four aspects of the Sphinx. The number twelve lies at the basis of the ancient Egyptian description of the great life cycle of the universe, the macrocosm, and of its microcosmic counterpart, the human soul. The macrocosmic cycle was referred to as the Great Year, the precession of the equinoxes; the microcosmic cycle of the soul was described as having twelve hours.[29]

Although the astronomical precession of the equinoxes corresponds to an historical period of 26,000 years, the cycle may equally well be understood as an archetype of consciousness evolution over time. The symbol thus applies to the overall movement of human consciousness over a period of 26,000 years as well as to the progression of an individual consciousness (or Initiation) within one lifetime. Following the precessional clock, the cycle of consciousness begins at hour zero which is also the twelfth hour. This is the hour of the androgyne, the hour of un-differentiation; it is a time where zero is equal to two. The Egyptians called this the "Great Equinox", the Greeks called it the "Alpha and the Omega"—the beginning and the end.

At the first hour emerges the primal duality of male and female, spirit and soul, human and bestial. The two opposite principles lie in a state of symbiosis. It is the hour of bliss where Adam and Eve dwell in perfect harmony in the Garden of Eden.

---

[29] The ancient Egyptians used a system by which twelve hours were attributed to the day and twelve hours to the night, indicating the dual nature of the cycle that takes place in the visible as well as in the invisible world.

The first hour is the Crater Cup or Cup of Forgetfulness into which the soul is plunged in manifested existence.[30] The spirit dwells within her, unawakened. The completion of the life cycle of consciousness, that is, the completion of the Great Work, requires the separation of the twin elements contained in the Cup. For only when separated are they able to polarise one another and thus give birth to an immortal "child" or "star". In so doing the Crater Cup is transformed into the Holy Graal.

In the precession cycle, the descent of the soul into the Crater Cup corresponds to the zodiacal sign of Cancer (♋) whose symbol expresses the intertwining of Sun and Moon, spirit and soul.[31] Cancer then represents the symbiotic condition of the twins at the beginning of existence. It is the condition of the natural soul, the first "Mary" who must be torn apart by the wheels of life so that the twin elements may work in polarity:

Let Mary inviolate be torn upon wheels: for her sake let all chaste women be utterly despised among you!

Liber AL vel Legis, III: 55

Thus and not otherwise she is able to beget the magical child who will transfigure her as the second "Mary", the Virgin of the 11th hour of the life cycle. As the Virgin, the soul is united with Hadit the Word or seed of pure consciousness symbolised by *The Hermit* of the Tarot.[32]

The Hermit or Virgin represents the soul freed from Leviathan and assumed into heaven by her magical child or star—as is recounted not only in the Christian legend but in tales of considerably greater antiquity. The rule of magical art, which the soul must follow to undergo this transformation, requires that she drink fully from the Graal or cup of blood given her by Hadit the life-giving spirit.

---

[30] The Crater Cup is described by Macrobius in Volume I of *Thrice Greatest Hermes*, translated by G. R. S. Mead.

[31] The number 6 is that of Tiphereth, the sephira of the Sun on the Hermetic Tree of Life; the number 9 is that of Yesod, the sephira of the Moon.

[32] The eleventh hour of the life cycle of consciousness corresponds to the zodiacal sign of Virgo, attributed to Tarot Atu IX, *The Hermit*.

In other words, the soul fully assimilates the 93 current of love under will. As the Virgin, the soul is "89", the Qabalistic number of "silence", "a body", and "bridal chamber"—and a talismanic formula.[33] The rules of this art are "eight and ninety" or 98; they are the soul's perfect opposite, her magical mirror. They are the means by which she unifies the animal, human and divine nature latent in her self:

There is help & hope in other spells. Wisdom says: be strong! Then canst thou bear more joy. Be not animal; refine thy rapture! If thou drink, drink by the eight and ninety rules of art: if thou love, exceed by delicacy; and if thou do aught joyous, let there be subtlety therein!

Liber AL vel Legis, II: 70

The immersion of the soul in the waters of the Crater Cup at the beginning of the life cycle is symbolised in the Gospel by the rituals of St. John the Baptist. The latter was born six months before Jesus; their respective births therefore coincide with the time of the summer and winter solstices.[34]

The summer solstice is the precise turning point between the astrological signs of Cancer and Leo. It is the depth of the Crater Cup, the baptismal font. The baptism conferred by John upon Jesus prepared and purified the latter for his ministry. That ministry was to initiate his disciples through a *second* baptism. The second baptism by spirit is what is called the Knowledge and Conversation of the Holy Guardian Angel.

---

[33] According to Aleister Crowley, the number 89 is "A number of sin—restriction: the wrong kind of silence, that of the Black Brothers". However, Crowley either ignored or was not aware of the vital talismanic formula that is implicit here. The body (GVP 89) is the tomb or mummy wrapping of the seed destined for the stars. The number is equal by Gematria to "sky", "heaven", and by Greek Qabalah it is equal to "bridal chamber" or "palace". When multiplied by the magick of eleven the result is 979. A Qabalistic investigation of 979 may yield much treasure. The number resumes the process of creating a magical child, a homunculus or Star of Nuit—a "Babe in the Egg of Blue".

[34] The annunciation to the Virgin Mary by the Angel Gabriel whereby the magical child Jesus was conceived by the power of the Holy Spirit took place in the *sixth* month of the pregnancy of Mary's cousin Elisabeth. The outcome of the latter resulted in the birth of John the Baptist (see Luke I).

In the Gospel, the baptism is called the second birth—a birth not of the flesh but of the spirit, through which the soul attains unity with the divine Word. As emphatically put in John, 3: 3–8:

"Verily, verily, I say unto thee, Except a man be born again, he cannot see the kingdom of God. Nicodemus saith unto him, How can a man be born when he is old? Can he enter the second time into his mother's womb, and be born? Jesus answered, Verily, verily, I say unto thee, Except a man be born of water and of the spirit, he cannot enter into the kingdom of God. That which is born of the flesh is flesh; and that which is born of the spirit is spirit. Marvel not that I said unto thee, Ye must be born again. The wind bloweth where it listeth, and thou hearest the sound thereof, but canst not tell whence it cometh, and whither it goeth: so is every one that is born of the spirit."

The baptism of St. John, the initiatory immersion of the soul in the Crater Cup, further symbolises the transmutation of the soul so that she may become a *Khu*, a vessel for the incarnation of new life and consciousness. The Knowledge and Conversation of the Holy Guardian Angel represents the birth of the magical child or star, the *Khabs*, in the *Khu* of the magically prepared Scarlet Woman or soul. The baptismal birth conferred by John must come before the birth by spirit, for as Nuit declares in Liber AL vel Legis, I: 8:

The Khabs is in the Khu, not the Khu in the Khabs.

The *Khabs* is always latent in the *Khu*, but this secret seed does not come to fruition unless the Great Work separates the twins intertwined in the original Cancerian symbiosis.[35] At the second hour the opposites separate from each other. They fall from symbiosis and are exiled towards the dawning of individual or solar consciousness. They establish a separate existence.

The biblical account of this phase of consciousness evolution is the story of Cain and Abel. Individual consciousness fully emerges at the third hour, arising from the darkness of un-differentiation as the sun rises from the darkness of night. To the fourth hour corresponds the maximum assertion of individual or dualistic consciousness. This fully externalises and objectifies the opposite principle.

---

[35] Note also that the astrological glyph of Cancer is "69", the Sun and Moon.

31

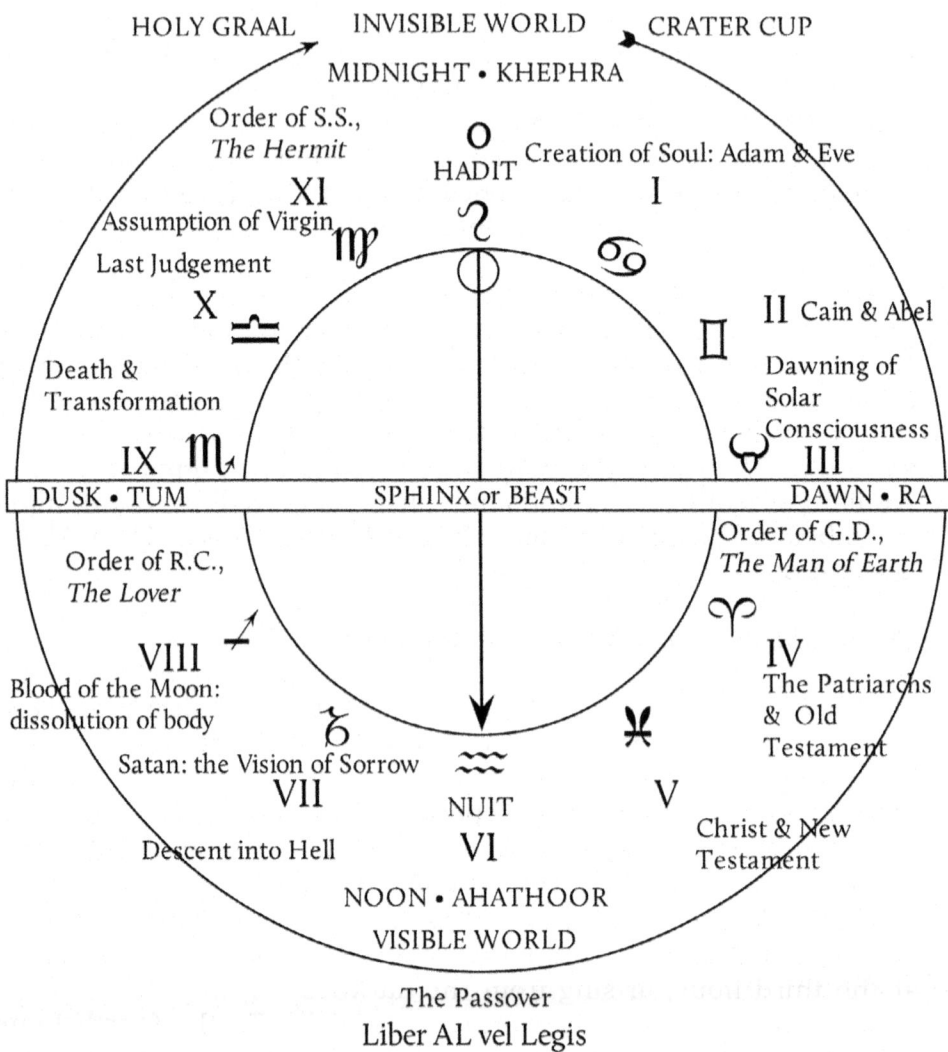

HOLY GRAAL   INVISIBLE WORLD   CRATER CUP

MIDNIGHT • KHEPHRA

Order of S.S.,
The Hermit

HADIT

XI

Creation of Soul: Adam & Eve

I

Assumption of Virgin

Last Judgement

X

II Cain & Abel

Dawning of
Solar
Consciousness

Death &
Transformation

IX

III

DUSK • TUM   SPHINX or BEAST   DAWN • RA

Order of G.D.,
The Man of Earth

Order of R.C.,
The Lover

VIII

IV

Blood of the Moon:
dissolution of body

The Patriarchs
& Old
Testament

Satan: the Vision of Sorrow

VII

NUIT

V

Descent into Hell

VI

Christ & New
Testament

NOON • AHATHOOR

VISIBLE WORLD

The Passover
Liber AL vel Legis

The fifth hour marks the beginning of the withdrawal of the projection that reached its apotheosis at the fourth hour. It marks the first movement towards the reconciliation of opposites.

The sixth hour, the exact mid-point of the cycle, corresponds to the time at which consciousness moves away from dualism. Solar, individual perception begins a descent towards death. It passes over from dualism, belief in that which consciousness is able to objectify, to non-dualism. This inevitably implies slaying the sense of self-identity that was acquired through the separation of opposites. Thus at the sixth hour there begins the way of return towards androgynous consciousness. There is much danger at this point, for there is a strong pull towards going back the way one came. This atavistic tendency naturally arises from the fear of death and the unknown experienced by individual consciousness that is facing what seems to be a spiritual crisis.

The seventh hour signifies the full descent into hell. This involves a confrontation with everything that has been dissociated from individual consciousness through the separation of opposites. Unless the atavisms arising from the unconscious depths can be overcome, the seventh hour is never passed. Instead of a return to eternity there is a regression and—ultimately—the possession by blind vampirical forces takes place. This is a considerable ordeal for the soul; unless she succeeds in assimilating the dissociated contents, these will in turn assimilate and destroy her.

The soul who passes through this ordeal reaches the eighth hour, the hour of dissolution. The opposites are now integrated and no enmity remains between them. The dissolution, however, is not a return to the primal symbiosis but is a move towards the synergy required to pass through death. Death, the ninth hour, is the hour of the transmutation of the elements of the physical body. The synergic interaction of matter and spirit is the key to the spiritual overcoming of death. Had the differentiation between them not taken place then these opposites would have remained incapable of the interaction that produces an effect greater than the sum of its separate parts. The combined effect is the Immortal Stone, arising at the end of the life cycle of consciousness.

The substance emerging from the ninth hour must then pass through the Last Judgement, the tenth hour where the aggregate consciousness of the soul is assessed. To pass through the Last Judgement, the soul must be found just. That is to say, the fruit of her experiences must conform to her True Will.

If the soul passes this judgement then she is brought to the eleventh hour. Here, she passes into eternity as a jewel in the heavenly body of Nuit. Shining as a diamond or star, her mutable substance has been fully transformed and is united with the imperishable, the immortal. The mysteries of the sixth and ninth hour were retold in the Gospels, where Jesus walks to the cross at the sixth hour and dies at the ninth:

"Now from the sixth hour there was darkness over all the land unto the ninth hour. And about the ninth hour Jesus cried with a loud voice, saying, Eli, Eli, lama sabachthani? That is to say, My God, my God, why hast thou forsaken me? Some of them that stood there, when they heard that, said, This man calleth for Elias. And straightway one of them ran, and took a sponge, and filled it with vinegar, and put it on a reed, and gave him to drink. The rest said, Let be, let us see whether Elias will come to save him. Jesus, when he had cried again with a loud voice, yielded up the ghost. And, behold, the veil of the temple was rent in twain from the top to the bottom; and the earth did quake, and the rocks rent; and the graves were opened; and many bodies of the saints which slept arose, and came out of the graves after his resurrection, and went into the holy city, and appeared unto many." (Matthew, 27: 45–53)

The three hours (ninth, tenth and eleventh) that the soul must pass to arise triumphant over death correspond to the three days that Jesus spent in the underworld before ascending into heaven. In Liber AL III: 34, the outcome of the great transfiguration is described via the perpetual metamorphosis of Ra, the Sun God. Having been born into terrestrial life as the "Hawk-headed mystical Lord", the Beast is able to send his life-giving spirit back into creation to arise as Hrumachis:

But your holy place shall be untouched throughout the centuries: though with fire and sword it be burnt down & shattered, yet an invisible house there standeth, and shall stand until the fall of the Great Equinox; when Hrumachis shall arise and the double-wanded one assume my throne and place. Another prophet shall arise, and bring fresh fever from the skies; another woman shall awake the lust & worship of the Snake; another soul of God and beast shall mingle in the globèd priest; another sacrifice shall stain the tomb; another king shall reign; and blessing no longer be poured To the Hawk-headed mystical Lord!

The Sphinx is the heart of the great cycle or clock that measures the life of the soul—as well as the movement of human consciousness throughout history. The date at which the Egyptian Sphinx was built is speculative, but at 10,000 BCE the constellation of Leo was rising (on the horizon) in the direction that the Sphinx is facing. If the Sphinx had existed at that vastly antique time then it would have been perfectly aligned with the polarity formed by Leo and Aquarius, or Hadit and Nuit.

The precession of the equinoxes follows the Zodiac wheel *in reverse* from the order in which the sun moves through the Zodiac throughout the year. If we suppose the Sphinx to represent the age of Leo then the latter represents the zero hour, midnight. The age of Taurus, for example, then corresponds to the third hour as the hour of sunrise. This is representative of the dawning of the consciousness that would evolve over the course of the Great Year initiated in the age of Leo.

In the present Great Year, the age of Taurus began in approximately 4000 BCE. During this age the unification of Egypt took place, and the beginning of what is referred to as the historical period—defined by the emergence of writing properly so called, in about 3000 BCE.

Another two thousand years or so brings us to the fourth hour, the beginning of the Age of Aries and the date at which Abraham is considered to have arrived in Canaan. The fourth hour thus historically corresponds to the era of the Patriarchs of the Old Testament. Half way through that age (c. 1230 BCE) Moses was said to have received the law at Mount Sinai. The year 2000 BCE also marks the beginning of Egypt's Middle Kingdom.

The fifth hour saw the beginning of the Christian era; the symbol of Christ is the fish, indicating the relationship between that phase of history and the astrological age of Pisces.

The age that we have now entered, Aquarius, represents the sixth hour, the beginning of the great return. It is fitting that Liber AL vel Legis should have been transmitted at the threshold of the Aquarian Age (called "Hrumachis" in the aforesaid book) for it deals with the soul's triumphant emergence from her descent in the underworld to pass into eternity or the Aeon of Horus. Thus she is able to return to the zero hour. Like the Word, the Sphinx is periodically lost under the desert sands. Major works of restoration of the Egyptian Sphinx have been undertaken on six occasions in history. The timing of these closely coincide with major events in the history of the divine covenance.

Thothmoses first restored the Sphinx around the year 1400 BCE at the beginning of the New Kingdom. It was at that time buried up to its neck in sand. Thothmoses had a dream in which the Sphinx asked him to free her from the sand, offering him as a reward the crown of Upper and Lower Egypt. This period of history coincides very closely with that of Moses reception of the law at Sinai that formed the basis of the old covenant.

The second restoration works took place in about 500 BCE when parts of the Sphinx were rebuilt. This coincides with the time of the end of the Kingdom of Judah and of the Egyptian Dynasties; it was around this time that Ankh-af-na-khonsu of the "Stele 666" was a priest in Thebes. The third restoration consisted of major excavation works undertaken by the Romans at the very beginning of the Christian era. It therefore coincided with the establishment of the new covenant.

The Sphinx was once more excavated in 1926, twenty-two years after the reception of Liber AL vel Legis. The 1926 works of restoration had severely damaging effects on the monument, as did the subsequent (fifth) restoration that took place between 1955 and 1987. These twentieth century undertakings could be considered as a particular manifestation of the anti-word of the Aeon of Horus. All manifestation takes place in duality—every thesis must have its antithesis. The anti-word disrupts and destroys order and harmony so that the reasoning faculty, for example, becomes cut off from heart or conscience. In the wider sense, the errors that have quite literally broken the heart of the Sphinx have resulted from the complete loss of Initiated spiritual knowledge from modern science and industry. It is only with the sixth and latest restoration work (1989 and ongoing) that the adverse effects of the twentieth century 'restorations' are being fully addressed. This is being done by an investigation aimed at a more complete understanding of the relationship between the monument and its environment.

Half way through a 26,000 years cycle of consciousness evolution mankind now stands on the threshold of the Way of Return. The human soul must resist the temptation of seeking to return to Eden by regressing into past modes of consciousness—for the latter results in the awakening of extremely dangerous atavisms that are impossible to control save by an Initiate with the appropriate keys. The Law communicated by Liber AL vel Legis calls the human soul forward, giving her the keys to self-polarisation and freedom. The Word of the Law is: Θελημα.

Chronological Table (precessional ages are approximate)

4000 BCE ♉	Beginning of the precessional Age of Taurus
3000 BCE	Beginning of the Historical Period Unification of Egypt as the Old Kingdom with Memphis as capital city The Canaanites; Abraham's ancestors as nomads in Mesopotamia
2000 BCE ♈	Beginning of the precessional Age of Aries Egypt: Middle Kingdom, approximately 2030–1720 Era of the Patriarchs, as described in Genesis 12–50 About 1850 BCE: arrival of Abraham at Canaan (Genesis 12) About 1700 BCE: the Patriarchs in Egypt
1500 BCE	Egypt: New Kingdom, 1560–715 with Thebes as capital city Thothmoses excavates the Sphinx at Giza Akhenaten (1377-1358) establishes exclusive worship of the Aten Tutankhamen (1358-1349) Seti l (1317-1301) Rameses ll (1301-1234) 1250–1230: Jewish Exodus, as according to the Bible 1230: Moses—the Law at Sinai, the Old Covenant
1000–500 BCE	1010–970: David 970–931: Solomon marries pharaoh's daughter and builds the Temple of Jerusalem 740: Call of the Prophet Isaiah 721–587: End of the Kingdom of Judah 663–525: XXVlth Egyptian Dynasty, last before Persian dominion; cult of Ankh-af-na-khonsu 627: Call of the prophet Jeremiah 622: Jewish Torah 'discovered' in the Temple of Jerusalem 604–562: Nebuchadnezzar, king of Babylon 600: Ezekiel predicts the ruin of Jerusalem 587: Capture of Jerusalem and destruction of the Temple and the city

37

538–333 BCE	500: Egypt: Restoration of the Sphinx on Giza Plateau Egypt: Restoration to Persian Period 525–400: Egypt: XXVIIth Dynasty—Persian domination 520–515: Building of the second Temple of Jerusalem 336–323: Alexander the Great
333–63 BCE	Hellenistic Period 331: Foundation of Alexandria
1 EV ♓	39–4 BCE: Reign of king Herod the Great 7 or 6 BCE: The chronicled birth of Jesus of the New Testament Roman Palestine Beginning of precessional Age of Pisces
63 BCE–135 EV	Egypt: The Romans excavate the Sphinx Autumn of 27 EV: Preaching of John the Baptist and the beginning of the ministry of Jesus Christ 30 EV: The death of Jesus on the eve of the Passover
1904 EV	Egypt: Reception of Liber AL vel Legis in Cairo on April 1st, 2nd and 3rd by Aleister and Rose Crowley ☉ ♈ ☽ ♎
1989 EV	Egypt: Latest restoration of the Sphinx—ongoing
2012–2016 EV ♒	Ending of the Great Cycle of the Aeons according to the Mayan calendar ☉ ♄ Solstice 2012 e.v. The Fall of the Great Equinox; full commencement of the Aeon of Hrumachis ☉ ♄ Solstice 2015 e.v.

The Chronological Table

1. We use the abbreviation BCE for "Before Common Era", and EV for Common Era (*era vulgaris*).

2. The Cairo Working, 1904 EV: In his published record of the working, Aleister Crowley thought to change the dates given for the reception of the Book of the Law to the 8th, 9th and 10th of April 1904—according to the writings of Kenneth Grant, who took notes from Crowley's diaries and holograph manuscripts while staying with the Beast at his Hastings lodgings (see the *Typhonian Trilogies*, Starfire Publishing). Crowley formally began the Cairo Working at the spring equinox, 20th March 1904 e.v. Magical operations frequently come to fruition at the full Moon; the reception of the Book of the Law would then have coincided with the three days of Easter on the 1st, 2nd and 3rd April. Easter is timed by the full Moon following the spring equinox. It is possible that Crowley might not have been comfortable with having the reception of a book proclaiming a new law for humanity dated to April Fool's Day and Easter, the most important Christian festival.

3. 2012–16 EV: The Capricorn solstice of 2012 e.v. coincided with the ending of the great cycle of the aeons, as according to the astronomical calculations of the Mayans. According to our scheme, based on the ancient Egyptian "First Time"—the Great Year commencing with the precessional Age of Leo the Lion at the end of the last ice age—the present time is that of the Fall of the Great Equinox (see the diagram, "Sphinx: Life Cycle of Consciousness", pp. 32). According to the prophetic elements in the third chapter of Liber AL vel Legis, the time would be marked by the burning down "by fire and sword" of Aleister Crowley's "Kiblah" or holy place, Boleskine Manor on the shores of Loch Ness. The event came to pass on the night of the winter solstice, 22nd December, 2015 e.v.

But your holy place shall be untouched throughout the centuries: though with fire and sword it be burnt down & shattered, yet an invisible house there standeth, and shall stand until the fall of the Great Equinox...

Liber AL vel Legis, III: 34

The History of the Divine Covenant

The Old Law

The recorded history of the covenant between man and God dates back thousands of years. The Western Tradition (so-called) which transmitted spiritual law through the ages originated in ancient Egypt and was continued to some extent by the Judaeo Christian religions. A fatal break in the continuity of that law or spiritual intelligence took place at the time when scripture superseded actual spiritual and psychic experience. This resulted in the wide-scale suppression and forcible abolition of the images of gods and their attributes that had for long ages acted as the magical keys to their invocation. Indeed, we are fortunate to have any images of art and architecture of the old world remaining with us at all, such was the fanatical zeal of the founders of what were to become the new world religions.[36]

With the breaking of this vital magical link a gaping fissure opened in human consciousness. With only man's reason to fall back on, the interpretation and dissemination of sacred texts was to become the weaponry by which power was wrested away from the gods—and ultimately, from God.

At the present time, scientific thought has largely usurped the power to shape ideas and culture that was once the domain of an army of theologians. Yet the old religions based on scripture still retain their emotive power. Caught between two blind alleys, each leading to a future either too dark to see or too bleak to contemplate, collective humanity and its industrial governors have, spiritually speaking at least, halted at the crossroads. In the magical work of Initiation, it is not possible to merely stop when a crossroads is reached—for the *karma*, or result of previous invocations, creates an irresistible force of momentum. One either continues to travel or self-destructs, sinking downwards to oblivion.

---

[36] Much of the written knowledge and history of the world was destroyed when the library of Alexandria burned down some time between the 2nd and 4th centuries EV (or CE). The rise of monotheism coincided with commencement of the enforced control and centralisation of religious worship by emerging nation states. Prior to monotheism, there was no word for "religion".

The symbolism used by the Intelligences who communicated Liber AL vel Legis to Aleister Crowley in 1904 may be found in the ancient Egyptian tradition as well as in the pages of the Bible. The keys of Liber AL vel Legis are Qabalistic, and so are many passages of the New Testament. Some of these were originally written in Greek, the language in which the word of the Law, Thelema, is given by Liber AL vel Legis. The word "thelema" is central to the Gospels (see Matthew, 6: 10 and 26: 42).[37]

The Qabalah sheds light on the meaning of St. John's prophetic book of Revelation. The latter introduces two of the central principles of Liber AL vel Legis: the Beast and the Scarlet Woman. Nuit is also alluded to in Revelation as "a woman clothed with the sun, and the moon under her feet, and upon her head a crown of twelve stars ... travailing in birth" (Revelation, 12: 1–2).

The woman who wears the crown of the zodiacal constellations is the great sign in heaven heralding the birth of the new Aeon of Horus the Crowned and Conquering Child of the Gods.[38] The woman of Revelation is also a representation of the fully initiated soul that has attained the consciousness of Hadit and whose magical child is her immortal "star". Therefore it may be helpful to approach Liber AL vel Legis armed with some knowledge of the history of redemption as it is presented in the Bible.

In the Judaeo Christian tradition, the beginning of the history of the divine covenant is recorded in the book of Genesis. History, in this context, is perhaps best understood as figurative rather than literal. It is very different from the concept of history as applied by modern historians. The absorbing concern of the narrators is the *meaning* of those historical events, events that flowered in time but are rooted in man's changing perception of himself. The tales are told as a series of events taking place in time—because this is how the human mind perceives things and remembers them. The details of such a narrative can only be understood when seen as part of a simultaneous whole, since the source is to be found in the depth of human consciousness. It is anchored in time and space by the attention given to it since the events unfold in consciousness each time the story is heard.

---

[37] The word "thelema" appears in the Greek version of these verses, where it is used for "will" in the phrase, "Thy will be done". That is to say, "Let not my personal will prevail, but the spiritual or True Will".

[38] The Aeon governed by the Law of Thelema is named after Horus, the Egyptian God of Resurrection and ruler of justified souls—those who have attained immortal life through power of the Word.

The symbolism used in biblical stories presupposes history; there existed no tension between the symbolic and the factual in the minds of the scribes. The book of Genesis gives an account of creation in which the male-female gods called the Elohim, a word usually translated in bibles as "God", first separate earth from heaven (see Genesis, 1). The book continues with the creation of man, which takes place in paradise (Genesis, 2). "Paradise" is clearly distinguished from "heaven" in the book of Genesis, though these are often confused. Paradise is the Garden of Eden or earth—but an earth that does not know either sin or death. In paradise, the God now named Tetragrammaton Elohim, usually translated as "Lord", fashions man of dust from the soil, breathes the breath of life into his nostrils and turns him into a living soul.[39] The book goes on to describe a primordial tragedy and its consequences for man.

The tragedy is the "original sin"—Adam and Eve's disobedience to their God, who commanded that they do not eat the fruits of the Tree of Knowledge of Good and Evil. They consequently fall from Eden, causing sin and death to enter into the world—for their God places a curse upon them and on the serpent that tempted them to disobey. He condemns them to suffering, sorrow and death (Genesis, 3: 14–19). Adam and Eve then conceive two children, Cain and Abel (Genesis, 4). Sin is passed through generation, and so pride and jealousy drive Cain to murder his younger brother. The blood of Abel cries out to God from the ground and God responds by condemning Cain to the life of a fugitive and wanderer over the earth. This punishment is too hard for Cain to bear, as he fears to be killed by whoever comes across him in his exile.

God then puts a mark on Cain to prevent anyone from striking him down. A few generations later the wickedness of mankind is so great that God comes to regret having made human beings on earth. He decides to flood the earth to destroy corrupted humanity and all living things, apart from the just man Noah with whom God makes a covenant: Noah and all the creatures he takes with him aboard the Ark which God commands him to build will be spared. Noah obeys. Saved from the flood he builds an altar to his God, who then promises never again to strike down every living thing as he had done in the flood (Genesis, 7: 19).

---

[39] Tetragrammaton Elohim Qabalistically designates Da'ath, uniting Chokmah and Binah. The Elohim were originally the *Gods*, male and female. The name of the monotheistic biblical demiurge Tetragrammaton (YHVH) was added to that of the Elohim in relatively modern times.

Time moves on and the descendants of Noah begin to people the earth (Genesis, 11). Throughout the earth, men still speak the same language and understand each other. As the tribes of Noah's sons move eastwards they settle in Babylonia and decide to build themselves a town with a tower that reaches up to heaven. God witnesses the pride and ambition of the sons of man and notices that they are a single people with a single language. To restrain their ambition, God confuses their language with the result that they no longer understand each other (Genesis, 11: 6). He scatters them all over the earth to prevent them from building the town that was called Babel because it was there that God confused the language of the whole earth.

The name "Babel" derives from the Hebrew root *bll*, that means, "to confuse". In Chaldean the name Babel means "Gate of the God". Theologians assert that because of man's pride, God no longer wishes him to form one body. Out of Babel or Babylon thus arise the spirits of multiplicity—the fragmentation of human consciousness.

Some further generations later, God continues the covenant with his people by making a promise to Abraham. Abraham was a patriarch blessed by the high priest Melchizedek—who is considered by some to be a risen master of the Order to which Christ would later belong. God tells Abraham that if he and his sons put their faith in him (rather than in themselves, as had done Adam and Eve when God tested them), their faith would save their souls from death by bringing them to an eternal kingdom or "promised land" (Genesis, 15: 6).

Abraham is then told by God, "I will bless those who bless you, and whoever curses you I will curse; and all peoples on earth will be blessed through you" (Genesis, 12: 3). Those who rely on faith are therefore promised by the God of the Old Testament to receive the same blessing as Abraham the man of faith. Yet between making this promise and fulfilling it by offering Abraham's sons the possibility of salvation through faith in Jesus Christ, their God gave them a law. The law that was—it is said—promulgated by angels and assisted by an intermediary called Moses is known (by Christian theologians) as the "old law".

The old Law of Moses laid the foundations for the vocation of a man fashioned in the image of God, prescribing what is essential to the love of God and neighbour. According to St. Augustine, "God wrote on the tablets of the law what men did not read in their hearts."

The prescriptions of the law are summed up in the Ten Commandments or Decalogue (Exodus, 20: 13 and Deuteronomy, 5: 17). According to Christian thinking, this law is holy and spiritual yet still imperfect. Like a tutor it shows what must be done but cannot give the strength or grace of spirit to fulfil it. Because of sin, which it cannot remove, it remains a law of bondage. Thus by giving the law to his people, God also places a curse upon them (Deuteronomy, 27: 26 and 28: 15).[40]

Without the old law—as the doctrine proposes—the people would not have known what sin was.[41] Enslaved by the power of the Beast or Leviathan they would never have known, it seems, the love and grace of the biblical god. This caused St. Paul to declare in his letter to the Romans (Romans, 7: 7) that it was not that the law itself was sinful; in itself, the law was holy since it expressed God's will. In short, the law in itself is powerless to provide salvation.[42]

No prescribed set of outward observances can prevent sin and death. In fact, the law makes it worse because although the law itself is not the source of sin, it becomes the instrument of sin by arousing concupiscence! By informing the mind it increases the "fault", which then becomes a conscious "transgression". The only remedy the old law can offer is punishment, curse, condemnation and death; hence it is called "the law of sin and death" (Romans, 8: 2).

Nevertheless it is supposed by theologians that the biblical God temporarily willed this system so as to allow people the chance to become conscious of their sin (fault or error), thereby to seek salvation solely in the grace of that God. It is self-evident that belief in any scriptural word of God as absolute truth is a conjuration that requires the most absurd mental gymnastics.

---

[40] The teaching of the Sapiental or Wisdom books (Job, Psalms, Proverbs, Ecclesiastes, Ecclesiasticus, Wisdom and Song of Songs) and the Prophets complete the Old Testament law. The book of Prophets set its course towards the new covenant.

[41] Certainly the ideas of sin and punishment for sin have been well drummed into human ears by rulers who desire to teach the masses a better way—usually in order to hasten the "flow of the economy".

[42] Thelemites may note that this word derives from "salve", an anagram of "slave".

The New Covenant (Christianity)

According to Christian theologians, when the time came to put an end to the old law the divine Word incarnated in the historical personage of Jesus Christ. By dying a sinner's death Jesus Christ satisfied the demands of the old law for a sacrifice, penalty or appeasement for the wrath of God.[43] At the same time it is supposed that Christ fulfilled all that was of positive value in the old law, emancipating the sons from the guardianship of the one who teaches them a better way (Galatians, 3: 25). With the advent of Christ the natural children of God are dead to the law and its curse—for Christ has redeemed them in order to make them live forever with their God through a process of adoption. Through his Holy Spirit he gives his disciples the inner strength to do what the law has prescribed. This order of grace, superseding that of the old law, may still be called a law but it is a law of faith in a man, a human being who is at the same time God and verily God, since he is the Son of God. The law of Christ is summed up in the New Testament, particularly the Sermon on the Mount (Matthew, 5–6).

The doctrine of the man who is a god and the god who incarnates in human flesh did not by any means arrive for the first time with the cult of Christianity. It is a retelling of much earlier myths and legends that can be found in sources all over the world. However, that case is very well documented. In the Initiated traditions that were in evidence long before the scribing of either the old or the new biblical covenants, the custom was for the priest to invoke the god into himself. This was done by various means; foremost of these is the method by which the priest assumes the image of the god. Having assumed to himself the god's image and attributes, the god was thus able to speak and even to act through the priest. There is a direct comparison here with the technique employed by Coptic Christian and Roman Catholic priests (if instructed) at the operation of the Eucharist. Christian doctrine requires that Christ be sent by God to free man from the curse that began with the sin of Adam, the "first man". Christ was the "second man" or man of heaven sent into the world to redeem the perishable soul of the first man, the man of earth (I Corinthians, 15: 45). By being cursed for man's sake and assuming the role of a sacrificial scapegoat for sin, Christ was said to effect his work of redemption.

---

[43] Previously, a goat was sacrificed to this God. It had all the sins of the people ritually conferred upon its head and was then thrown over a precipice to its death. Needless to say, the sacrifice had to be made repeatedly, since men continued to sin!

The Bible says, "Cursed is everyone who is hanged on a tree" (Deuteronomy, 21: 23). The curse is echoed—albeit strangely—in Liber AL vel Legis, chapter III, verses 50–53:

Curse them! Curse them! Curse them!

Horus denounces all world religions since their followers are bound to the word(s) of the old aeon (Pisces by precession). As such they are blinded by Horus and cannot see their way through the New Aeon; belief no longer commands salvation. We have now arrived in the present and perhaps, in the future too. The triple curse is delivered against the multiplicity, fragmentation and confusion engendered by all written down words of law. It reverses the curse placed by the biblical God upon mankind when it tried to reach for heaven by building the tower of Babel. The curse pronounced by Horus the God of the New Aeon destroys sin by destroying division itself. Only a universal language—*not* written—ensures the continuation of beauty, truth and spiritual knowledge. As such, the curse spelled out in Liber AL vel Legis reopens the "Gate of the God", Babel, to draw multiplicity back to a source that cannot be directly expressed in any verbal sense.[44] According to the writings of Kenneth Grant (in his *Typhonian Trilogies*), this has grave implications for humanity since the resurgence of primeval atavisms from the deep unconscious—or their counterparts in the depths of cosmic space—is an inevitable consequence. Without the keys of Initiation, man is defenceless against the reawakened and vampirical un-dead.

The Ending of the Words: Thelema

The biblical account of the history of redemption is presented in narrative form. In Liber AL vel Legis the elements are *transmitted* from a level beyond ordinary speech and sight. The divisive tales told by the major religions of the world all sprang from the immense power of textual narratives. Liber AL vel Legis is thus:

The ending of the words...

Liber AL vel Legis, III: 7

---

[44] Babel or Babylon is also Babalon, a name sometimes given to the Scarlet Woman of Liber AL vel Legis. Her "Fifty Gates" are the sum of the sephiroth below Da'ath, or "Knowledge".

46

According to the Law of Thelema, the eternal is divided for love's sake and for the chance of union. Such is the life of the soul uniquely identified with the bipolar zero of the unfragmentary body of Nuit:

For I am divided for love's sake, for the chance of union. This is the creation of the world, that the pain of division is as nothing, and the joy of dissolution all.

Liber AL vel Legis, I: 29–30

The curse placed upon mankind as a consequence of its separation from God is spoken of in Liber AL vel Legis, I: 52 as the direful judgements of Ra Hoor Khuit:[45]

If this be not aright; if ye confound the space-marks, saying: They are one; or saying, They are many; if the ritual be not ever unto me: then expect the direful judgments of Ra Hoor Khuit!

But when Nuit chooses, the aspirant dies to division. According to Liber AL vel Legis, III: 1, such a death brings him the reward of Ra Hoor Khuit: Abrahadabra, the Holy Graal or *Khu* body that is at once conterminous with the infinite body of Nuit:

Abrahadabra; the reward of Ra Hoor Khut.

The Initiate thus forges a bridge, doorway or crossing that leads out of the world created by the word of Sin that is Restriction and towards freedom:

The word of Sin is Restriction. O man! refuse not thy wife, if she will! O lover, if thou wilt, depart! There is no bond that can unite the divided but love: all else is a curse. Accurséd! Accurséd be it to the aeons! Hell.

Liber AL vel Legis, I: 41

---

[45] Ra Hoor Khuit is the Holy Spirit aspect of the Trinity who speaks through chapter three of Liber AL vel Legis. The feminine identity of Nuit now supersedes the All-Father of monotheistic religious cults. The Son (and lover) of Nuit is named Hadit.

In the final book of the Bible, St. John's Revelation, the ultimate betrayer of God's love is portrayed as the famous prostitute Babylon, who embodies the sins of the whole world. When Babylon falls, a gateway is reopened that destroys confusion and multiplicity, or sin. This brings about the gathering of all the nations in heaven; it is the prerequisite to the coming of the kingdom of heaven (Revelation 19). Only after his death as the accursed Scarlet Woman is Jesus able to ascend to heaven, there to dwell forever as Christ.

Some writers have asserted that Christ was really a woman. Perhaps the best example of Christ as Scarlet Woman—and the resultant double irony—is found in the work of Félicien Rops in his 1878 painting, *Temptation of Saint Anthony* (see pp. 50). While studying an illuminated manuscript depicting a voluptuous illustration for "The Land of Joseph", the saint sees a leering devil dressed in a scarlet robe hurling the corpse of Jesus—the Word—from the Cross. In place of the inscription "INRI" appears the word "EROS". Loosely bound rather than nailed to the Cross stands a voluptuous, naked, flaming-haired woman in full bloom of beauty. The snout of a hairy pig—a creature sacred to Set or Satan—points in the direction of her genitalia. The torsos of the attending cherubs have turned into horrid skeletal demons. Most notable of all is the fact that the whole scene appears to be taking place on a Golgotha that has been transformed into a mountain of huge books! Thus the living spirit of the New Aeon comes to destroy the dead letter of the Word.

The Surrealist Salvador Dali found much to inspire as well as to amuse him in the revulsion and horror experienced by the saints when confronted with the female anatomy. His version of *Temptation of Saint Anthony* (1946) is darkly suggestive of the possibilities for perverted revelry in the contemplation of any object of projected sin, shame and humiliation.[46]

While Jesus is made to drink vinegar and gall at his crucifixion (Matthew 27: 34), the Babylon of Revelation is made to drink a full wine cup of God's anger before her fall (Revelation, 16: 19). Liber AL vel Legis gives the key of freedom from the bondage of all dualistic conceptions of sin and death. The soul of the prophet has to unite with the serpent that gives knowledge to mankind—the Beast who "once was and is not and is yet to come up from the Abyss, but only to go to his destruction" (Revelation, 17: 8).

---

[46] Max Ernst also painted the subject—with unbridled demonic ferocity—in 1945. Dali and Ernst may also have been inspired by earlier works, such as that of Matthew and the Angel in the *Gospel Book of Archbishop Ebbo of Reims.*

The Beast's dualistic power of projecting his identity and the primordial utterance that undoes this conception of the self are one and the same. In Liber AL vel Legis, the identities of Adam and Christ—that is, 'fallen' and 'arisen' consciousness—are merged in the identity of the Beast, a single consciousness moving through different phases of creation. The force or power of the Beast that brings about the fall of creation from paradise is shown here to be the means of returning to it. The masculine solar force of the Beast is embodied in his feminine counterpart, referred to in Liber AL vel Legis as the Scarlet Woman. She is Eve whose name means "Life", the life of Adam or the Beast. She is the natural soul or biblical woman of sin and is identical to the great whore Babylon of St. John's Revelation. As life, she is indeed the "Gate of the God", the door through which the Beast passes in and out of creation.

As with the Beast, Liber AL vel Legis merges the fallen and risen aspects of the Scarlet Woman into one identity. There is an obvious reference, though, to the biblical and theological notion of purity from sin that is only possible through chastity in the literal sense—thus rendering nature as sinful and evil in itself:

Let Mary inviolate be torn upon wheels: for her sake let all chaste women be utterly despised among you!

Liber AL vel Legis, III: 55

The soul or Scarlet Woman is warned against the confused notion that *spiritual* chastity (or faithfulness) implies a universally applicable moral code to be 'lived up to'. As the book has it, "thou hast no right but to do thy will" (Liber AL vel Legis, I: 42). Liber AL establishes that creation, fall and eternity represent one perpetual continuum of living consciousness:

Now ye shall know that the chosen priest & apostle of infinite space is the prince-priest the Beast; and in his woman called the Scarlet Woman is all power given. They shall gather my children into their fold: they shall bring the glory of the stars into the hearts of men.

Liber AL vel Legis, I: 15

The Temptation of Saint Anthony by Félicien Rops (1878)

Christ said: "And I, if I be lifted up from the earth, will draw all men unto me" (John, 12: 32). The destruction of the fallen Beast of St. John's Revelation inevitably reinforces dualistic conceptions of the triumph of good over evil. The Scarlet Woman of Liber AL vel Legis, however, destroys the pain of division to make way for the joy of dissolution. In Liber AL vel Legis, III: 45, it is said that her achievement "will lift her to pinnacles of power":

Then will I lift her to pinnacles of power: then will I breed from her a child mightier than all the kings of the earth. I will fill her with joy: with my force shall she see & strike at the worship of Nu: she shall achieve Hadit.

Transformed by the power of the Beast she is able to gather her chosen devotees into her fold and so "bring the glory of the stars into the hearts of men". Aleister Crowley saw himself, rightly or wrongly, as the first prophet chosen to proclaim the Law of Thelema on earth:

To each man and woman that thou meetest, were it but to dine or to drink at them, it is the Law to give. Then they shall chance to abide in this bliss or no; it is no odds. Do this quickly!

Liber AL vel Legis, III: 39

Crowley's magical workings and publishing efforts brought to focus the rationalist, humanist creed *Deus est Homo*—"God is Man". The thrust of nineteenth and twentieth century thought has been to explain all phenomena in rational terms. Unthinking acceptance of *Deus est Homo* automatically leads to reductionism and the psychologising of the symbolism of the mysteries. This was intended to be a step away, however, from the crippling paralysis induced by religious and other doctrines.

Symbolism—the special language of the mystery traditions—has always served to veil truth not comprehensible to the ordinary human mind, at the same time opening a secret path to its apprehension for those who have learned and understood the keys or magical correspondences. Mystical texts such as "The Mystical Flame of Love" (St. John of the Cross) consist of very sensual imagery. Liber AL vel Legis is not unique in this since it resumes the romance in the language of the Prophet and Bride:

For he is ever a sun, and she a moon. But to him is the winged secret flame, and to her the stooping starlight.

Liber AL vel Legis, I: 16

Unfortunately, once every man is declared as being his own God it is then difficult to support the argument for arduous training in a spiritual discipline, as Aleister Crowley subsequently discovered. Nonetheless the Great Work of Initiation in all ages has necessitated the training of the personal will so that it may act as a receiver and transmitter for the still voice that is outside and beyond the human personality. When this transmutation is fully accomplished then Horus the Avenging Angel of Death becomes the Crowned and Conquering Child of the Gods. Horus is the Egyptian god of resurrection who is at one and the same time the guardian of imperishable souls, or stars, and the scourge of the wicked and profane. In the first century of the historical Aeon of Horus the Great Work has concerned destruction and re-absorption of the living consciousness of the previous aeon. This was inevitable since the vast magical influx of energy or "blood" into the New Aeon could not otherwise find expression in human consciousness.

The legends of the birth and childhood of Horus all include an account of his being stricken with poisoning by his dark double, Set or Satan—the Lord Initiating—and brought near to death. The condition of Horus while in the paralysed state, on the threshold of death and neither in this world or the next, is typical not so much of the birth of a New Aeon as of the chaotic interval *between* aeons. The birth of Horus was in secret, according to the tale that was once taught to Egyptian children. His reign was not established by the fact of his birth alone. Once he has survived the poisoning—which is made of all the ills that afflicted the consciousness of the old aeon plus the collective fear of the unknown piled up against the incoming magical current—then he is able at last to perfect his word in Maat or Truth. It may be that the initial phase of the Great Work of the Aeon of Horus has been accomplished. The voiceless echoes of the anti-word of Liber AL vel Legis reveal a disillusioned mankind struck dumb and blinded with the horror of its impossible condition. There is a spiritual vacuum even where the religions of the previous aeon continue to flourish. The negativity created by the absence now evident where the Word once flowered is everywhere the prevailing mode.

52

The initial destructive phase of the Great Work is now superseded by a constructive—yet silent—aeon.[47] When Horus is made Maat then his unceasing battle against Set becomes a play of love between stars. The trajectory of each star following the course of its True Will is such that in its wake the deathless constellations are stirred and churned in a peculiar manner. From the cauldron of the working, brimful of the luminous foam of the stars, is dropped forth the dew of new worlds to come—as yet unexplored and unknown by man or Beast. Of course the "war in heaven" or fight for the soul goes on being frightfully enacted on earth. Thus the Aeon of Hrumachis is truly double, "two and none". Initiates have traditionally walked to and fro between the worlds. Now they are to accomplish this with infinite subtlety:

Be not animal; refine thy rapture!

Liber AL vel Legis, II: 70

Thelemites, freed from material illusion, will know the love and delights of the innermost senses as declared by Nuit:

I love you! I yearn to you! Pale or purple, veiled or voluptuous, I who am all pleasure and purple, and drunkenness of the innermost sense, desire you. Put on the wings, and arouse the coiled splendour within you: come unto me!

Liber AL vel Legis, I: 61

Liber AL vel Legis only abolishes the law of love and faith in the outward sense; the inner sense and meaning of these is fulfilled by the complete uniting of the faithful to the beloved in Nuit who gives "certainty, not faith" (Liber AL vel Legis, I: 58). The motion towards internalising and being assumed by the Law of Thelema is thus complete, and the perfect universality of the latter is reflected in its perfect application to the particular. To love others as one loves oneself is then no longer questionable, as it was in the writing of the New Testament: one has *become* the others. To the disciples of Thelema that are moved beyond the curses of the old covenants and their ill-founded promises, divine law becomes:

---

[47] We are not speaking here of the Aeon being constructive in any material sense.

Ultimate sparks of the intimate fire.

Liber AL vel Legis, III: 67

Nuit calls through her son, her manifested star, to the three powers of the soul: her Will, her Understanding and her Memory. The Great Work takes place under the direction of Hadit, who exhorts the soul thus:

Remember all ye that existence is pure joy; that all the sorrows are but as shadows; they pass & are done; but there is that which remains.

Liber AL vel Legis, II: 9

The apparently sorrowful or fallen condition of the universe is, after all, illusionary. The soul is nonetheless initiated by the vision of suffering and death as this provides the necessary conditions for her spiritual awakening.[48] She will be led by Hadit through her own death and resurrection so as to open a portal or gateway through which others may pass to discover new worlds of beauty and truth. Such portals are, however, completely invisible to the world of ordinary senses. The value of initiatory ordeals is not in the suffering itself, which is finite, but in the soul's infinite desire for the love of Nuit—a desire that springs from Nuit herself.

Liber AL vel Legis came into the world at a time in which human reason had declared God dead. As Erich Fromm wrote in *The Sane Society* in 1955:

"In the nineteenth century the problem was that God is dead; in the twentieth century the problem is that man is dead."

---

[48] The Book of the Law differs from Buddhism, which declares, "Existence is sorrow". Buddhism admits the sorrow to be the result of ignorance or illusion, but it cannot see existence other than in negative terms. Christian theology calls this "original sin", whereas the Book of the Law states: "The word of Sin is Restriction" (I: 41). The dependence on the translation of the Word into codified rules and moral precepts is the root of the 'sinful' error.

In killing the truth man destroys himself. However, the Thelemic transmission or 93 current does not allow human reason to prevail against love.

The more modern antecedents of Thelema include some of the works of Nietzsche, especially *Thus Spake Zarathustra*. It does not seem altogether improbable that the "93" transmission spawned the Surrealist movement that produced its manifesto in 1924—twenty years after the reception of Liber AL vel Legis. Nietzsche, the Book of the Law and the Surrealists declared war on reason, the "word of Sin" (Liber AL vel Legis, I: 41). This does not require that reason and intelligence be discarded altogether. It does require that the armour-plated dogs of reason be silenced. As Aleister Crowley wisely put this in *The Book of Thoth*: [49]

"Heed not the siren-voice of sense, or the phantom voice of reason: Rest in simplicity, and listen to the silence."

In Liber AL vel Legis, II: 28–33, Hadit, the son of Nuit and her Word, warns the Adept against the folly of rationalism:

Now a curse upon Because and his kin!
May Because be accurséd forever!
If Will stops and cries Why, invoking Because, then Will stops & does nought.
If Power asks why, then is Power weakness.
Also reason is a lie; for there is a factor infinite & unknown; & all their words are skew-wise.
Enough of Because! Be he damned for a dog.

The book often takes on a vindictive tone; its similarity to the language used by Old Testament prophets such as Ezekiel or Daniel in their eschatological writings cannot fail to be noticed. The Stele of Revealing belonged to a priest of the cult of Ankh-af-na-khonsu who lived at the time of the XXVIth Egyptian dynasty. The dynasty extended between the years 663 and 525 BCE, a time during which the history of Egypt became increasingly merged into that of the Middle East and Greece. The priest of the Stele of Revealing was a contemporary of Ezekiel and of the events described at the beginning of the book of Daniel.

---

[49] The subject of Aleister Crowley's oracular verse is Tarot Atu VI, *The Lovers*, corresponding to Gemini and signifying dualistic reason.

This period of history coincides with the end of the Kingdom of Judah, which culminated with the Babylonian capture of Jerusalem and the destruction of the Temple in 587 BCE. Ezekiel predicted the events in around the year 600 BCE shortly after the supposed deportation to Babylon—a time at which the Temple had been taken over by "pagan cults".[50]

It was at this time (622 BCE) that the priest Hilkiah faked the rediscovery of the Jewish Book of the Law or Torah (2 Chronicles, 34: 14 or 2 Kings, 22: 8).[51] The priest of the cult of Ankh-af-na-khonsu therefore received the eschatological revelation recorded on his Stele at the apotheosis of an age. The end of the Kingdom of Judah marked the beginning of a tumultuous period that paved the way for the messianic era.[52]

The work of Ezekiel, written at the time when the Ankh-af-na-khonsu cult flourished in Thebes, marked a critical turning point in the history of Judaism. The style of Ezekiel bears many similarities to that of Liber AL vel Legis. Like Ankh-af-na-khonsu, Ezekiel was both a priest and a prophet—something unusual in Judaism. Ezekiel broke with tradition in many ways; he asserted the principle of individual rather than collective retribution. He is considered to be the first Hebrew prophet to approach the theology of "grace" later developed by St. John and St. Paul.[53]

Liber AL vel Legis dismisses the theology of redemption with an uncompromising treatise concerning the supremacy of infinite love over human reason, and the unpredictability of the Holy Spirit which "bloweth where it listeth" (John, 3: 8)—incarnating the Word in a new form in every age. Now the Word is to withdraw in Silence, as humanity has been informed that its own reason is a lying spirit. Mankind totters on the brink of extinction amidst unseen emanations that shape his destiny according to cosmic forces he is unaware of—since he does not see, hear or feel them.

---

[50] The original use of the term "pagan" was derogatory, and referred generally to illiterate peasants of no fixed abode. In this case it refers to any cult that was not that of Yahweh or Jehovah. Christian writers use it to indicate any non-Christian cult.

[51] There is evidence that Hilkiah—a tax collector—did this for political reasons.

[52] After the end of the Kingdom of Judah came the restoration in which a second temple was built, then the Persian period which ended in 333 BCE when the Hellenistic period began. The Romans took over in 63 BCE. Palestine remained under Roman rulership until 135 EV.

[53] Aleister Crowley confused the notion of spiritual grace—the descent of the Holy Spirit—with its psychological equivalent in his ritual, "The Mass of the Phoenix".

From the chaos of a new dark age Liber AL vel Legis shines a light that is invisible save to those enraptured by the love-song of Nuit. The latter will ultimately encounter Hadit as an initiatory trial or ordeal:

I am the flame that burns in every heart of man, and in the core of every star. I am Life, and the giver of Life, yet therefore is the knowledge of me the knowledge of death.

Liber AL vel Legis, II: 6

For the soul who endures the ordeals of the path of knowledge, heaven may be known both during and after earthly existence:

I give unimaginable joys on earth: certainty, not faith, while in life, upon death; peace unutterable, rest, ecstasy; nor do I demand aught in sacrifice.

Liber AL vel Legis, I: 58

The spiritual pulse of Thelema is love, while its wisdom is only known through discernment—which is the essential discipline of the path of knowledge:[54]

Love is the law, love under will. Nor let the fools mistake love; for there are love and love. There is the dove, and there is the serpent. Choose ye well!

Liber AL vel Legis, I: 57

---

[54] The path of knowledge, implicit in many passages of Liber AL vel Legis, is called *Ynana Yoga* in the Eastern tradition—see the works of Swami Vivekananda, the foremost disciple of the mystic Sri Ramakrishna.

"Behold, I send an Angel before thee, to keep thee in the way, and to bring thee into the place which I have prepared. Beware of him, and obey his voice, provoke him not; for he will not pardon your transgressions: for my name is in him. But if thou shalt indeed obey his voice, and do all that I speak; then I will be an enemy unto thine enemies, and an adversary unto thine adversaries."

Exodus, 23: 20–22

The Western Tradition includes the idea that from the beginning of time God made two orders of creatures. These consisted of the spiritual order and the corporeal order—the angelic and the earthly. At the centre of creation was placed the human creature that partakes of both orders, since he is composed of body and spirit. "Angel" is the name of the office of the spiritual creatures. The name comes from the Greek word *angelos*, which means, "a messenger". By nature, angels are spirits that are servants and messengers of God—those "that excel in strength, that do his commandments, hearkening unto the voice of his word" (Psalms, 103: 20). As purely spiritual creatures, angels have intelligence and will. They are both personal and immortal creatures. From infancy to death human life is surrounded by the intercession of the angels: "Beside each man and woman stands an angel as shepherd leading them to life" (St. Basil). In the words of St. Matthew's Gospel, 18: 10:

"Take heed that ye despise not one of these little ones; for I say unto you, that in heaven their angels do always behold the face of my Father which is in heaven."

The angels mentioned in the Bible were derived in the main from the Egyptian *Neteru*—gods that embodied natural principles as well as earth locations, or *chakras*.[55]

---

[55] The ancient Egyptians called the inner earth or body locations *nomes*; in the Eastern Tantras these are called *chakras*. There may be an etymological link here with the gnomes or earth spirits of folklore—the dwellers in the deep or subterranean hollows. With the passing of time, the spirits 'below' were all identified with the Devil and therefore thought to be evil or at best, mischievous.

The *Neteru* became translated through the scriptural writings of later cults into the myriad angels, thrones, dominions, principalities and saints.[56] According to scriptural writing, the angels were involved in the fall, so-called. Behind the disobedient choice of Adam and Eve lurks a seductive voice that is opposed to the will of their God and which makes them suffer death out of envy.[57] The scriptures view this voice as that of a fallen angel called Satan or the Devil, whose fall alludes to the exercise of the free choice of some of the created spirits.[58]

Unlike Adam and Eve, whose disobedience was somewhat passive in the biblical narrative, the fallen angels radically and irrevocably rejected God and his reign. A reflection of the heroic spirit of rebellion is found in the words that Satan addressed to Adam and Eve: "You will be like God(s)" (Genesis, 3: 5). The word that is commonly translated as "God" here is "Elohim". This is better translated as "Gods, male and female". In the Hebrew Qabalah, the divine name Elohim also refers to a particular office of angels—a plurality of holy spirits.[59] According to the Gospel of St. John, 8: 44, the Devil "has sinned from the beginning"; he is "a liar and the father of lies." In this context the Devil is the originator of the illusion of separation, and therefore of suffering and death, the condition of man after the fall. According to Liber AL vel Legis, the separation is necessary and vital since it is the very essence of creation:

For I am divided for love's sake, for the chance of union. This is the creation of the world, that the pain of division is as nothing, and the joy of dissolution all.

Liber AL vel Legis, I: 29–30

The Western Hermetic Tradition presupposes that the solution to suffering and death rests upon man's ability to obtain union with the Word of God. The natural soul pertains to creation that, owing to the original sin, is fallen and in a state of separation from the eternal.

---

[56] See E. A. Wallis Budge, *The Gods of the Egyptians.*

[57] See Genesis, 3: 1–5 and Wisdom, 2: 24.

[58] See John, 8: 44 and Revelation, 12: 9.

[59] The Elohim ("Gods") are the Order of Angels usually attributed to Netzach the seventh sephira (Venus) on the Tree of Life, while the Beni Elohim ("Sons of the Gods") correspond to Hod the eighth sephira (Mercury).

To unite with the divine Word the soul requires the mediation of one capable of acting as a messenger between her world and eternity. The Word may then be incarnated in the soul and born therein. The soul is then born a second time, by spirit. The spiritual child begotten by the soul will assume her in his own wisdom and immortality:

"I tell you most solemnly, unless a man is born through water and the spirit, he cannot enter the kingdom of God: what is born from the flesh is flesh; what is born from the spirit is spirit." (John, 3: 5–6)

If the soul should neglect the Great Work of the magical child, then she and her child may suffer the fate of annihilation. The warning concerning the work of the Holy Guardian Angel is delivered through the voice of Ra Hoor Khuit, the Angel of judgement and death:

Let the Scarlet Woman beware! If pity and compassion and tenderness visit her heart; if she leave my work to toy with old sweetnesses; then shall my vengeance be known. I will slay me her child: I will alienate her heart: I will cast her out from men: as a shrinking and despised harlot shall she crawl through dusk wet streets, and die cold and an-hungered.

Liber AL vel Legis, III: 43

Thelema curses the "word of Sin", the errors and confusion that are piled up higher than the tower of Babel as a result of fixing the Word in doctrines that are as rigid as the corpse of Jesus on the Cross. There is nonetheless a Great Work to be done. This is only possible through a messenger or bridge between the worlds that is known to the practitioner of Hermetic art as the Holy Guardian Angel, for:

There is no law beyond Do what thou wilt.[60]

Liber AL vel Legis, III: 60

---

[60] Do what *thou* wilt—not, "do what ye will"!

It is integral to the doctrine of the Western Tradition that every human being born into this world has a counterpart in the invisible world. The implication conveyed to us through such remnants of ancient wisdom as *Thrice Greatest Hermes* is that the presence of the Angel (or *Daemon*) is blotted out of consciousness by the rational mind. The child that is born out of the soul crippled by reason is death. The magical impregnation or irradiation by the 93 current is then abortive and so the soul cannot participate in the joy promised by Nuit to her chosen ones.

It will be seen at once that the aims of Thelema cannot be confused with the quest for personal freedom and individual self-expression that characterises the ideals of "the people"—and the advertising industry. The achievement of the soul outlined in Liber AL vel Legis depends on vital magical and spiritual factors. Far from being a type of spiritually sanctioned hedonism, as some would have it, Thelema requires the soul to apply ruthless discrimination on the path. This is made all the more difficult since only the knowledge of the True Will conveyed by the Holy Guardian Angel can provide the guiding truth for each soul—yet the spiritual work to be done has profound import to every man and every woman that is a star. The choice for the soul is still understood to be one of life on the one hand or annihilation on the other.

Several stories of the Old and New Testaments testify to the double nature of man and to the mysteries of the Holy Guardian Angel—the spiritual counterpart, lover, brother, double or devil of the natural soul. One such story is that of Cain and Abel, narrated in the Book of Genesis (Genesis 4). After the fall (Genesis 3), Adam and Eve conceive a first child with the help of God. His name is Cain, which in Hebrew means "possession", as well as "spear".[61] They then conceive a second child, Abel, whose name means "breath". The story of Cain and Abel can be understood as a metaphor for the birth of man as a double being. Cain represents the physical life, and Abel the spiritual life or Holy Guardian Angel.

---

[61] The Hebrew root of the word "spear" means "fixity". The name "Cain" is therefore linked to that of "Set" that has the meaning, "to fix in place". The Book of Genesis (4: 25–26) goes on to tell us that after Cain and Abel, Adam and Eve gave birth to another child by the name of Seth, granted to them by God to replace Abel—whom Cain had killed.

Abel grows up to be a shepherd, an image for the keeper of souls that refers to the earlier tradition of Hermes Trismegistus.[62] Cain on the other hand is a tiller of the soil. Both brothers make offerings to God, who gracefully accepts the offering of Abel while rejecting the offering of Cain. The offerings made by Abel were of the spirit while those of Cain were of earth or flesh. Cain is much angered by God's rejection of his offering. God then warns Cain that his ill-disposed temperament will prevent him from remaining master of himself. Perhaps the warning was more in the nature of prophecy than advice—for Cain tells his brother to go out with him and, once in the open country, he kills him. The "open country" may here refer to the outside world, the world entered by the soul at birth. In physical birth the soul is forgetful. The spirit is "killed" then by the natural tendencies of the soul, ego or earthly part of man. In the story, the spilled blood of Abel then cries out of the ground and God punishes Cain by condemning him to a life of exile. Thus begins the life of man exiled from eternity by the severance of the bond with his spirit.

Cain is terrified by this punishment, as he believes that anyone he meets will want to kill him. In an act of grace, God places a mark on Cain to protect him. A sevenfold vengeance will be taken for Cain if anyone strikes him down. The mark in question is that of the Holy Guardian Angel, Abel. His protection is sevenfold since he dwells in the world that is ruled by seven sacred spirits of life before the throne of God. Cain then leaves the presence of God and settles East of Eden in the land of Nod. The latter name is rooted in the word "nad" that means "wanderer". This can also be taken to mean sleep, forgetfulness or dispersion of mind and will.

The story of two brothers representing complementary aspects of one man may also be found in the story of the twins Jacob and Esau (Genesis, 25: 23). As the twins fight in the womb, God tells their mother Rebecca:

"There are two nations in your womb, your issue will be two rival peoples. One nation shall have mastery over the other, and the elder shall serve the younger."

---

[62] The title of Hermes as the "good shepherd" was later borrowed by the Christians who, not surprisingly, attributed it to their own divine personage, "Jesus".

Esau, the older brother, will have to give up his birthright to his younger brother. The attribution of the man of earth to the older brother and man of spirit to the younger is mirrored in the relationship between John the Baptist and Jesus in the Gospel. John and Jesus are born of two cousins, Mary and Elisabeth (Luke, I), who both miraculously conceive with the help of the Holy Spirit after an annunciation by the Angel Gabriel.[63] John is born first as he will be the witness of Jesus, of whom he says: "He who comes after me ranks before me because he existed before me" (John, I: 15). There is clearly a parallel between the blood of Abel that cries out of the ground to God and the blood later shed by Jesus to redeem the sins of the entire world—as according to Christian theology. It is the blood pouring out of the wound inflicted by man upon his spirit. It is the magical seal placed upon the covenant of redemption.

In the book of the prophet Ezekiel (Ezekiel, 41: 19), the inside of the Hekal or Hall of the Temple is described as being adorned with cherubs having two faces, the face of a man and the face of a lion. These represent the spiritual and the corporeal aspects of man. The man or angel, and the beast or lion, correspond to the zodiacal signs of Aquarius and Leo. The two signs are the polarity ruling the present astronomical age governed by the Law of Thelema. The conjunction of these opposites takes place in the second chamber of the Temple described by Ezekiel. The Initiate who passes through this chamber, that is, who unites with his Holy Guardian Angel, may attain to the knowledge symbolised by the third chamber of the Temple, the Holy of Holies.[64]

In Liber AL vel Legis, the Holy Guardian Angel or spiritual counterpart of man is referred to by its Egyptian name, the *Khabs* ("star"). The star is latent until it emerges into the consciousness of the natural soul. Made conscious, it becomes the soul's aspiration to spiritual knowledge. The incarnation of the Word of the True Will within the *Khabs* fertilises it. The *Khabs* is then able to manifest as a magical child whose body is called the *Khu*.

---

[63] The annunciation is made to Mary in the case of the birth of Jesus, and to Zechariah the husband of Elisabeth in the case of John the Baptist.

[64] The Temple described by Ezekiel has three parts, called the *Ulam* or Vestibule, the *Hekal* or Hall (the Holy), and the *Debir* or Sanctuary (the Holy of Holies). It is an almost exact replica of the Temple of Solomon described in Kings, I: 6.

The substance of the *Khu* body is extracted or distilled from the substance of the soul herself. Without the body provided by the natural soul the *Khabs* could not develop into a fully autonomous spiritual being. In other words the magical child grows out of the substance of the soul—not the soul out of the substance of the magical child. The magical child then ultimately assumes the entire substance of the soul as his own body. As Liber AL vel Legis puts it:

The Khabs is in the Khu, not the Khu in the Khabs.

Liber AL vel Legis, I: 8

The soul who then worships the *Khabs*, that is, who gives all her blood or energy to the Graal cup of Babalon—her magical child—receives from that child the knowledge of Nuit:

Worship then the Khabs, and behold my light shed over you!

Liber AL vel Legis, I: 9

Such is the story of the incarnation of Jesus in the womb of Mary. The only difference is that religious doctrine insists this must be a one-time-only event whose operation depends entirely on historical authenticity. At the Egyptian centre of Aunnu (Heliopolis) thousands of years before the time of the historical Jesus, the birth of a god named Horus from the womb of a Virgin called Isis was celebrated. At Aunnu, Horus was uniquely revered as a double deity named Heru-Set.[65] Using an analogy between spiritual and physical generation one would equate the following principles: the natural soul is as the womb; the *Khabs* is then an egg in the womb. The Word fertilising the egg (thus doubling it) is as the spermatozoon. The *Khu* is the child's body that grows by receiving nourishment from his own mother, the soul. In the physical world the continuity of existence takes place through successive generations, each of which is subject to death. In the spiritual world the continuity of existence takes place through the immortalisation of the mother-soul through her child or star.

---

[65] The biblical account of Christ's temptation by Satan continues the much earlier Egyptian narrative concerning the trials of Horus by Set.

64

Liber AL vel Legis was transmitted to Aleister Crowley by his Holy Guardian Angel, Aiwaz. Throughout Liber AL vel Legis, Aiwaz does not speak on his own behalf. He is the hearer of the Word and the communicator of it to the soul. Through Aiwaz the voices of a trinity of Egyptian gods speak forth, revealing their mysteries to creation. Aiwaz holds the title of "minister of Hoor-paar-kraat" (Liber AL vel Legis, I: 7). On numerous occasions Aleister Crowley describes Hoor-paar-kraat (Harpocrates in Greek) as "the babe in the egg of blue".[66] The Babe of the Abyss is the latent child, the Holy Guardian Angel or "dwarf self" of Hinduism, who comes to birth when the egg or *Khabs* is fertilised by the Word called Hadit in Liber AL vel Legis. He is the child of silence, the silence in which the soul must enter to hear the Word, incarnate it, become it, and thereby pass into eternity. Aiwaz is the messenger sent to reveal this sacred magick:

Behold! it is revealed by Aiwaz the minister of Hoor-paar-kraat. The Khabs is in the Khu, not the Khu in the Khabs.

Liber AL vel Legis, I: 7–8

The *Khabs* is known in the language of the alchemist as the philosophers stone. In Greek, the word for "stone", *psephos*, also means, "a voice". This is revealing of the relationship between the philosophers stone or *Khabs* and the Word, a relationship referred to in St. John's Revelation, II: 17. Here, Christ asks St. John to write to the angel of the church in Pergamos and say:[67]

"He that hath an ear, let him hear what the spirit saith unto the churches; To him that overcometh will I give to eat of the hidden manna, and will give him a white stone, and in the stone a new name written, which no man knoweth saving he that receiveth it."

No man knows the new name or Word of the Aeon because this name is Hadit, who is the Knower. But he may realise his true nature as a *Khabs*, a perfect expression of that Word. He may then partake of the knowledge of Hadit.

---

[66] In particular, see *The Vision and the Voice* by Aleister Crowley.
[67] Pergamos means "height" or "elevation".

A French magical grimoire translated into English at the end of the nineteenth century by S. L. MacGregor Mathers, founding member of the Hermetic Order of the Golden Dawn (1888–1900), contains a great deal of information on the magical operation known as the "Knowledge and Conversation of the Holy Guardian Angel". The book, entitled *The Book of the Sacred Magic of Abramelin the Mage*, contains precise Qabalistic instructions on how to contact one's Holy Guardian Angel, and was delivered by a magician called Abramelin to his son Lamech in the year 1458. The particular system of magick advocated in that book is rooted in the biblical doctrine regarding creation, the fall, and the double nature of man who is both a spiritual and a corporeal creature. It is concerned with the role of man in the redemption of creation through incarnation of the divine Word. As explained by Mathers in his introduction to Abramelin's book, the Great Work of redemption is based on a dualistic conception:

a) That the Good Spirits and Angelic Powers of Light are superior in power to the Fallen Spirits of Darkness.

b) That these latter as a punishment have been condemned to the service of the Initiates of the Magic of Light.

c) As a consequence of this doctrine, all ordinary material effects and phenomena are produced by the labour of the Evil Spirits under the command usually of the Good.

d) That consequently whenever the Evil Demons escape from the control of the Good, there is no evil that they will not work by way of vengeance.

e) That therefore sooner than obey man, they will try to make him their servant, by inducing him to conclude Pacts and Agreements with them.

f) That to further this project they will use every means that offers to obsess him.

g) That in order to become an Adept, therefore, and dominate them, the greatest possible firmness of will, purity of soul and intent, and power of self-control is necessary.

h) That this is only to be attained by self-abnegation on every plane.

i) That man, therefore, is the middle nature, and natural controller of the middle nature between the Angels and the Demons, and that therefore to each man is attached naturally both a Guardian Angel and a Malevolent Demon, and also certain Spirits that may become Familiars, so that with him it rests to give the victory unto which he will.

66

j) That, therefore, in order to control and make service of the Lower and Evil, the knowledge of the Higher and Good is requisite.

Mathers sums up the work as follows:

"From this it results that the *magnum opus* propounded in this work is: by purity and self-denial to obtain the knowledge of and conversation with one's Holy Guardian Angel, so that thereby and thereafter we may obtain the right of using the Evil Spirits for our servants in all material matters."

Obtaining the Knowledge and Conversation of the Holy Guardian Angel is therefore the prerequisite to doing the Great Work. Without it, man is spiritually ignorant; his interaction with spirits is not in conformity with his True Will, but is directed by his Evil Genius to lead him to destruction. The Evil Genius is the root of separation from the love of Nuit, as she warns the Adept in Liber AL vel Legis, I: 52:

If the ritual be not ever unto me: then expect the direful judgements of Ra-Hoor-Khuit!

In times of great change, such as the commencement of a New Aeon, the question of whether or not to renounce one's religion may arise. The advice given by Abramelin is wise enough to provide a partial answer to this question, but the working out—as exemplified by the full commentary given by Mathers—requires some manipulation! A more complete answer to this question is supplied by Liber AL vel Legis. Here, the Thelemite is to overcome the limitations of the traditional religious outlook—which is divisive as each religion makes its own claim to the truth. He does this not by denying the truth of any particular religion but by transcending the limiting doctrines that have grown up around all of them, freezing religion in time and making it as rigid as a corpse. Ra Hoor Khuit, Lord of the Aeon of Horus, announces that he is himself to be a "blasphemy against all gods of men", who defiantly tells mankind:

I spit on your crapulous creeds.

Liber AL vel Legis, III: 54

The Last Judgement

But your holy place shall be untouched throughout the centuries: though with fire and sword it be burnt down & shattered, yet an invisible house there standeth, and shall stand until the fall of the Great Equinox...

Liber AL vel Legis, III: 34

Human consciousness inhabits a world ruled by finality. Man's knowledge of the eternal, where beginning and end are realised as simultaneous, unfolds between the marks of the beginning and the end of time. The Initiation of the soul in time is punctuated by the events that prepare her for a final confrontation with truth and reality. The soul that is in love with her Holy Guardian Angel undergoes transmutation and passes into eternity; divided from him she goes her own way, loses substance and perishes. All spiritual traditions identify such a confrontation—be it called the Last Judgement, the Day of the Lord, Ordeal x or simply "death"—as the ultimate trial of the soul at the crossroads of Initiation:

I am the visible object of worship; the others are secret; for the Beast & his Bride are they: and for the winners of the Ordeal x.

Liber AL vel Legis, III: 22

Liber AL vel Legis is a book of the dead in so far as the mystery it reveals is that of the ultimate ordeal. It is also a book of life. The key of life is the relationship of the soul with the Holy Guardian Angel—by which she may emerge triumphant from Ordeal x.

Eschatological writings are found throughout the books of the Bible, particularly among the books of the Prophets, in sections of the discourses of Jesus Christ recorded in the Gospels, in various Epistles of the New Testament and in St. John's Revelation. A consistent pattern runs through these scriptures. They describe the soul's confrontation with evil that tests her spiritual integrity, fortifies her, cleanses her from sin or error and prepares her for eternal life. The spiritual confrontation with death includes the experience named "the abomination of desolation" by the prophet Daniel and Jesus (Daniel, 9: 27 and Matthew, 24: 15).

The eschatological discourse recorded in the Gospel according to St. Matthew (24: 1–31) describes this great tribulation as a time when the deceptions of the world—called *Maya* or "world illusion" in the East—will tempt the soul. She is thus led away from the Word and the possibility of redemption. The soul capable of overcoming these deceptions will be redeemed by her faith in the Word, who will gather her elements into his own spiritual life.

Understood in alchemical terms, the abomination of desolation is a descent into hell through which the soul is to encounter, consume and transmute the elements of her own being and raise herself triumphant in a regenerated, immortal body or *Khu*. The elements that she is to assimilate in her descent into Hades will destroy her if she is cut off from the Holy Guardian Angel (and therefore her True Will). Putting that another way, she may fall prey to the seduction of sensory illusions (or "false prophets").

Ra Hoor Khuit, the third person of the Thelemic Trinity, directly relates the Book of the Law to this ordeal. Concerning the funeral stone or stele of the cult Initiate named after the prophet Ankh-af-na-khonsu, Ra Hoor Khuit informs us:

That stélé they shall call the Abomination of Desolation...

Liber AL vel Legis, III: 19

The first biblical reference to the abomination of desolation is recorded in the twelfth chapter of the book of Daniel. Twelve is the number of the completion of the life cycle of consciousness represented by the precession of the equinoxes. The book of Daniel is the last and most direct expression of messianic prophecy in the Old Testament.[68]

The book of Daniel bears many similarities to the book of Ezekiel. Ezekiel and Daniel were both contemporaries of the Egyptian Initiatic cult of Ankh-af-na-khonsu. They were prophets of the end of an age, heralding a 'crossing over' into a new consciousness.[69] They asserted the doctrine of the angels.

---

[68] The book of Daniel was probably completed in its present form at the end of the persecution said to take place between 167 and 164 BCE.

[69] The book of Daniel begins with a description of events said to take place at the time of the Babylonian King Nebuchadnezzar. See the Chronological Table (pp. 37).

With its "sealed book" (12: 4), its message for generations to come and its deliberately enigmatic style, the book of Daniel is closely related to that of Revelation. In the latter, the seals of the closed books are broken (Revelation, 5–6) and its words are secret no longer. This is because the coming of the Lord is expected and "the time is at hand" (Revelation, 22: 10). The books of Daniel and Revelation both paved the way for the mysteries of the Last Judgement expounded in Liber AL vel Legis. A study of the twelfth chapter of the Book of Daniel is helpful so we can understand the relationship between Daniel's abomination of desolation and the funeral stele of an Ankh-af-na-khonsu priest in Thebes:

1. And at that time shall Michael stand up, the great prince which standeth for the children of thy people: and there shall be a time of trouble, such as never was since there was a nation even to that same time: and at that time thy people shall be delivered, every one that shall be found written in the book.

2. And many of them that sleep in the dust of the earth shall awake, some to everlasting life, and some to shame and everlasting contempt.

3. And they that be wise shall shine as the brightness of the firmament; and they that turn many to righteousness as the stars forever and ever.

4. But thou, O Daniel, shut up the words, and seal the book, even to the time of the end: many shall run to and fro, and knowledge shall be increased.

5. Then I Daniel looked, and, behold, there stood other two, the one on this side of the bank of the river, and the other on that side of the bank of the river.

6. And one said to the man clothed in linen, which was upon the waters of the river, How long shall it be to the end of these wonders?

7. And I heard the man clothed in linen, which was upon the waters of the river, when he held up his right hand and his left hand unto heaven, and sware by him that liveth for ever that it shall be for a time, two times, and an half; and when he shall have accomplished to scatter the power of the holy people, all these things shall be finished.

8. And I heard, but I understood not: then said I, O my Lord, what shall be the end of these things?

9. And he said, Go thy way, Daniel: for the words are closed up and sealed till the time of the end.

10. Many shall be purified, and made white, and tried; but the wicked shall do wickedly: and none of the wicked shall understand; but the wise shall understand.

11. And from the time that the daily sacrifice shall be taken away, and the abomination that maketh desolate set up, there shall be a thousand two hundred and ninety days.[70]

12. Blessed is he that waiteth, and cometh to the thousand three hundred and five and thirty days.[71]

13. But go thou thy way till the end be: for thou shalt rest, and stand in thy lot at the end of the days.

Verse 2 (above) is one of the key texts of the Old Testament on the resurrection of the body. The resurrected body is the *Khu* spoken of in Liber AL vel Legis, the magical body in which the Initiate may pass into the company of heaven at the end of time. Verse 3 refers to "the vault of heaven", the body of Nuit or company of heaven, and the transformation of the Initiates who will be "as bright as stars for all eternity". In verse 4, Daniel is told that he "must keep these words secret and the book sealed until the time of the End". It was only at the "time of the End"— the ending of the words—when the Law of Thelema would be given to mankind, that the seal would be opened:

Come! all ye, and learn the secret that hath not yet been revealed.

Liber AL vel Legis, II: 2

The opening of the sealed book is central to the Revelation of St. John (Revelation, 6) in which the Lamb breaks open the seven seals. There, as in Liber AL vel Legis, the word "come" or "be with us" is uttered as the seals of knowledge are opened. "Come" is Hadit's invitation to pass into the company of heaven as well as an expression of Nuit's love chant, "To me! To me!" (Liber AL vel Legis, I: 65).

In verse 6, Daniel then asks: "How long shall it be until the end of these wonders?" The answer is: "it shall be for a time, two times, and an half".

---

[70] 1,290 is expressed by the Hebrew letters Aleph, Resh, Tzaddi—or, ARTz (291), "Earth".

[71] 1,335 is written Aleph, Shin, Lamed, Hé—or, ShALH (336) "attack; request or petition".

Three and a half is the number of coils of the two serpents entwined around the Staff of Hermes. "Three and a fraction" is also an expression of *Pi*, the ratio between the circle—the body of Nuit or electron cloud—and the diameter formed by the opposite principles of spirit and soul, Beast and Scarlet Woman, proton and neutron.[72] *Pi* is therefore the number of the synergetic energy bringing about the birth of a magical child by the squaring of the circle. Three and a half is the number of the *Kundalini*, the power of the Beast who rises at the end of time, "that was, and is not ... and goeth into perdition" (Revelation, 17: 11). It is the Beast who carries the Scarlet Woman to her doom, the doom of Ordeal x also described in Revelation 18: 10:

"Alas, alas, that great city Babylon, that mighty city! for in one hour is thy judgment come".

This is echoed in Liber AL vel Legis, I: 61, where Nuit says to her prophet:

For one kiss wilt thou then be willing to give all; but whoso gives one particle of dust shall lose all in that hour.

The Scarlet Woman in this context is the natural soul, the material universe that will be destroyed when the Serpent Power of the Beast arises, fusing objective and subjective states of consciousness. The name burning on the foreheads of those who have climbed to the top of the Mountain of Initiation is Hadit, the Serpent Wonder:

Burn upon their brows, o splendrous serpent!

Liber AL vel Legis, I: 18

Aleister Crowley spelled the name of the Scarlet Woman BABALON, since this adds Qabalistically to 156. The number 156 is equal to 13 multiplied by 12, and some of Babalon's mysteries are concealed in the thirteen verses of the twelfth chapter of Daniel. Transmuted into an immortal *Khu* after her fall or Ordeal x, she is the heavenly Jerusalem seen by St. John and described in Revelation, 21: 1–5:

---

[72] *Pi*—see the Appendices, "The Master Key of Thelemic Atomic Correspondences".

"And I saw a new heaven and a new earth: for the first heaven and the first earth were passed away; and there was no more sea. And I John saw the holy city, New Jerusalem, coming down from God out of heaven, prepared as a bride adorned for her husband. And I heard a great voice out of heaven saying, Behold, the tabernacle of God is with men, and he will dwell with them, and they shall be his people, and God himself shall be with them, and be their God. And God shall wipe away all tears from their eyes; and there shall be no more death, neither sorrow, nor crying, neither shall there be any more pain: for the former things are passed away. And he that sat upon the throne said, Behold, I make all things new. And he said unto me, Write: for these words are true and faithful."

World renewal is the outcome of the completion of the life cycle of consciousness; it is the Holy Graal. The new heaven and new earth are the life of the company of heaven promised by Nuit to her chosen:

This shall regenerate the world, the little world my sister, my heart & my tongue, unto whom I send this kiss.

Liber AL vel Legis, I: 53

The transmutation of the Scarlet Woman—comparable to the body or host broken and eaten at a Mass—is described in the Acts of the Apostles (10: 9–16) where Peter receives a vision revealing that the soul must consume that which is deemed impure so as to become an incorruptible vessel—an instruction often echoed in the Eastern Tantras:

"Peter went up upon the housetop to pray about the sixth hour: And he became very hungry, and would have eaten: but while they made ready, he fell into a trance, and saw heaven opened, and a certain vessel descending unto him, as it had been a great sheet knit at the four corners, and let down to the earth: Wherein were all manner of four-footed beasts of the earth, and wild beasts, and creeping things, and fowls of the air. And there came a voice to him, Rise, Peter; kill, and eat. But Peter said, Not so, Lord; for I have never eaten any thing that is common or unclean. And the voice spake unto him again the second time, What God hath cleansed, that call not thou common. This was done thrice: and the vessel was received up again into heaven."

In Liber AL vel Legis, Ra Hoor Khuit conveys to the prophet instructions for this alchemical operation, telling him:

The best blood is of the moon, monthly: then the fresh blood of a child, or dropping from the host of heaven; then of enemies; then of the priest or of the worshippers: last of some beast, no matter what. This burn: of this make cakes & eat unto me. This hath also another use; let it be laid before me, and kept thick with perfumes of your orison: it shall become full of beetles as it were and creeping things sacred unto me. These slay, naming your enemies; & they shall fall before you.

Liber AL vel Legis, III: 24–25

The monthly blood of the moon is the outpouring of the blood or energy of Hadit—the Serpent Power—upon the soul that has survived the ordeals at the "end of time". Timing is the essence in all operations of magick, as with operations of alchemy. By periodicity, the marking of time or "space marks", the magician utilises the subtle emanations or vital elixirs to infuse the soul or Scarlet Woman. She may then become a vehicle capable of melting the bars on the cage of linear time. By these emanations or "thick perfumes of your orison" the bounds of time and space are suspended. Through the *Shakti*, as Babalon is called in the Tantras, an invisible web or subtle network extends "faery light" by which dew drops of immortality are precipitated. Along the luminous fibres woven into the masks assumed by the Magus and his double or counterpart, beads of light may pass to and from other worlds or dimensions of reality. The transmutation of the flesh or Scarlet Woman into a spiritual body or *Khu* at the end of time is also described in Ezekiel (47: 1–2) where the prophet, in a vision, is led by an angel to the gate of the Temple of Jerusalem, the "heavenly Jerusalem" later described by St. John in Revelation.

"Afterward he brought me again unto the door of the house; and, behold, waters issued out from under the threshold of the house eastward: for the forefront of the house stood toward the east, and the waters came down from under from the right side of the house, at the south side of the altar. Then brought he me out of the way of the gate northward, and led me about the way without unto the utter gate by the way that looketh eastward; and, behold, there ran out waters on the right side."

The prophet is led through ever-deepening waters until they are so deep he can no longer cross them. The measurer of the line or Word then tells him that these are veritably the waters of life proceeding to the east, to the desert, and into the sea, and that as even the sea thereby shall be healed, so shall any creature that is touched by the waters of life. Fishermen shall then stand upon the water and cast their nets, catching as many kinds of fish as according to the kind of the fishermen. However, as according to Ezekiel, 47: 11–12:

"But the miry places thereof and the marshes thereof shall not be healed; they shall be given to salt. And by the river upon the bank thereof, on this side and on that side, shall grow all trees for meat, whose leaf shall not fade, neither shall the fruit thereof be consumed: it shall bring forth new fruit according to his months, because their waters they issued out of the sanctuary: and the fruit thereof shall be for meat, and the leaf thereof for medicine."

The Temple described by Ezekiel is the body of the Adept stretched on the cross of the four elements (North, South, East, West) and passing through the waters of time and space to the Last Judgement or astrological Age of Aquarius. The torrent represents the outpouring of the spirit, blood or energy of Hadit that grows wider and deeper, broadening through the vast expanse of consciousness represented by the sea. The fishermen are the souls of all those who are immersed in the 93 current; the fishes and creeping things are the corruptible elements to be transmuted by it. Those who do not, or are not able to "abide in this bliss" (Liber AL vel Legis, III: 39) are therefore turned into "sterile salt-pits", bereft of the waters of life. They are caught in the trap of the Word as scripture, science or the law of man's reason—static and cursed to atrophy. Ezekiel reveals that the cross, crossing point or abomination of desolation is the means by which the eternal draws creation back to itself. The cross or Tau is the symbol of Saturn or Time. The winning of Ordeal x gives consummate meaning to all man's magical dealings with angels, gods or other supernatural beings:

For I am divided for love's sake, for the chance of union. This is the creation of the world, that the pain of division is as nothing, and the joy of dissolution all.

Liber AL vel Legis, I: 29–30

According to Ra Hoor Khuit, Lord of the Last Judgement:

I am the Lord of the Double Wand of Power; the wand of the force of Coph Nia—but my left hand is empty, for I have crushed an Universe; & nought remains...

There is a splendour in my name hidden and glorious, as the sun of midnight is ever the son. The ending of the words is the Word Abrahadabra.

Liber AL vel Legis, III: 72 & 74–75

"Abrahadabra" is the reward of Ra Hoor Khut (Liber AL vel Legis, III: 1); it is the incorruptible body granted to the soul who has been justified at the hour of Judgement, as according to the Egyptian tradition.[73] The ordeal of the abomination of desolation is the prerequisite of what Judaism calls the Passover—the passing over from one world to the next. It was at the Jewish festival of the Passover—the celebration of the supposed crossing of the Red Sea lead by Moses—that Judas betrayed Christ. There followed Christ's passion, crucifixion and resurrection; that is, his own ordeal and passing over. The celebration of the final Passover meal between Christ and his disciples became known as the Last Supper, and marked the institution of the Eucharist or Christian Mass. In the Gospel of St. Luke, 22: 7–13, the following details are recorded concerning the preparations of the Last Supper:

"Then came the day of unleavened bread, when the passover must be killed. And he sent Peter and John, saying, Go and prepare us the passover, that we may eat. And they said unto him, Where wilt thou that we prepare? And he said unto them, Behold, when ye are entered into the city, there shall a man meet you, bearing a pitcher of water; follow him into the house where he entereth in. And ye shall say unto the good man of the house, The Master saith unto thee, Where is the guest-chamber, where I shall eat the passover with my disciples? And he shall shew you a large upper room furnished: there make ready. And they went, and found as he had said unto them: and they made ready the passover."

---

[73] The heart is balanced in the scales of Maat when the word is perfectly expressed or uttered. See E. A. Wallis Budge, *The Gods of the Egyptians*, Volume 1, Chapter XIII, "Thoth and Maat".

The Last Supper will be eaten in a house to which a man, "bearing a pitcher of water", will lead the disciples. The man in question refers to the astrological glyph for the Age of Aquarius. This happens to coincide with the historical Aeon of Horus in the form of Hrumachis or Hormaku.[74] On the Hermetic Tree of Life, the path of Aquarius extends from Tiphereth to Chokmah and crosses the Abyss of Da'ath—the crossing, Passover, or "place of no return".

Liber AL vel Legis conveys to the Initiate the spiritual law of the Last Judgement—though this is emphatically not a codified set of moral rules or "commandments". The soul that has passed through the Ordeal x by the power of Ra Hoor Khuit has thereby achieved Hadit. The question of the necessary transformation of the forces of evil and death undergone by the soul is addressed thus:

But let her raise herself in pride! Let her follow me in my way! Let her work the work of wickedness! Let her kill her heart! Let her be loud and adulterous! Let her be covered with jewels, and rich garments, and let her be shameless before all men! Then will I lift her to pinnacles of power: then will I breed from her a child mightier than all the kings of the earth. I will fill her with joy: with my force shall she see & strike at the worship of Nu: she shall achieve Hadit.

Liber AL vel Legis, III: 44–45

This verse has sometimes been interpreted by Aleister Crowley and his followers as though it presented us with a literal feminine role model. However, in the context of Thelemic Initiation, the soul's "work of wickedness" is to have defeated the dogs (or gods) of human reason. She is "loud" for she has uttered the Word of her True Will, thus exorcising the demonic forces that enthral humanity in its susceptibility to 'reasonable' manipulation. Her "adultery" consists of the willed betrayal of her marriage to all that binds the uninitiated to time and death, choosing instead to pursue her affair with her Holy Guardian Angel. Hence her shamelessness before all men: the soul no longer fears the rejection or disapproval of the "many and the known" (Liber AL vel Legis, I: 10) who, under the spell of the dogs of reason, will fall under the direful judgment of Ra Hoor Khuit and become as sterile as salt-pits. The path—and its difficulty—is revealed.

---

[74] See the chapter, "The Aeon of Hrumachis or Horus-Maat" (pp. 78).

The writer Kenneth Grant—who studied the holograph manuscripts and diaries of Aleister Crowley while staying with him at his retirement home in Hastings—testifies to the likelihood that Crowley received the three chapters of Liber AL vel Legis on the 1st, 2nd and 3rd April 1904, which coincided with the three days of Easter that year—as opposed to the 8th, 9th and 10th as Crowley later claimed. The coincidence between the reception of Liber AL vel Legis and the three days of Easter that are rooted in the tradition of the Passover is supported by the words of Ra Hoor Khuit, who tells the prophet:

That stélé they shall call the Abomination of Desolation.

Liber AL vel Legis, III: 19

The soul who has realised Nuit has realised her self as conterminous with the rest of creation; she therefore partakes in the joy of the world as opposed to the deceptive comforts and weak desires of the "slaves of Because". In Liber AL vel Legis, II: 21, Hadit declares:

We have nothing with the outcast and the unfit: let them die in their misery. For they feel not. Compassion is the vice of kings: stamp down the wretched & the weak: this is the law of the strong: this is our law and the joy of the world.

Uncompromising instructions are also given by Ra-Hoor-Khuit:

Mercy let be off: damn them who pity! Kill and torture; spare not; be upon them!

Liber AL vel Legis, III: 18

This refers to the attitude that the soul must adopt in order to overcome the pull of her elemental nature or *Ka,* and so become a suitable vehicle for the Word of her True Will. Although the dualistic trap of the "holy covenant" of old times is now superceded by the *unwritten* Law of Thelema, there is in all times a war in heaven to be enacted upon earth for the soul who would be the winner of "Ordeal x". In other words, there is a Great Work yet to be done.

The Aeon of Hrumachis or Horus-Maat

The Great Aeon exists both inside and outside of time. Outside of time he is an eternity whose celestial body or *Khu* is illuminated by his *Khabs*, his head or intelligence. Inside of time he is a polymorphous god whose various aspects come to life for limited periods. During each phase a particular *type* of consciousness becomes prevalent on earth as part of the life cycle of consciousness. This is symbolised by the precession of the equinoxes—for the mutable, historical face of the Great Aeon corresponds to the astrological ages. The ages are the shadows or earthly twins of their eternal counterpart. They are sub-abysmal projections of their timeless double—divided for the chance of union, for the sake of love.

The earthly twin of the eternal Aeon of Horus is the astrological Age of Aquarius ruled by the planet Saturn. The Age of Aquarius signifies the arising of Hrumachis at the "fall of the Great Equinox" (Liber AL vel Legis, III: 34). The formula of Horus traditionally includes the twin aspects of Hoor-paar-kraat and Ra Hoor Khuit. While Hoor-paar-kraat watches over the aeon in eternity, Ra Hoor Khuit projects it forwards and in time. He thus manifests the aeon *in time*. Hoor-paar-kraat and Ra Hoor Khuit are identical to the brothers Set and Horus who were called by the ancient Egyptians, "he who is above" and "he who is below".[75] The Egyptians pictured the polar twins as standing (Horus) and sitting (Set). Horus and Set form the vertical and horizontal axes of the Aeonic Cross that squares the Great Wheel of the Aeons. The consciousness manifested by the 93 current in the Age of Aquarius or Aeon of Hrumachis is Saturnian or *Neschemic*. It is the consciousness of Nuit that transcends the duality of lunar and solar consciousness. The 93 current reveals the unity of earth and heaven, matter and spirit, or son and mother, equating "two" with "zero":

O Nuit, continuous one of Heaven, let it be ever thus: that men speak not of Thee as One but as None; and let them speak not of thee at all, since thou art continuous! None, breathed the light, faint and faery, of the stars, and two. For I am divided for love's sake, for the chance of union.

Liber AL vel Legis, I: 27 29

---

[75] See E. A. Wallis Budge, *The Gods of the Ancient Egyptians*, Vol. II (pp. 243).

The Egyptians attributed the planet Saturn to Horus, and the planet Mercury to Set. The Aeon of Hrumachis is therefore both Saturnian and Mercurial: Saturn rules over the consciousness of the Aeon; Mercury governs its incarnation in time and the magical transmutation of the incarnated units of consciousness. The power of Set sent forth in creation is Ra Hoor Khuit, the martial god of the Serpent Power.[76] In Liber AL vel Legis III: 72, after the "fall of the Great Equinox" (III: 34), Horus becomes "Lord of the Double Wand of Power". Liber AL vel Legis is the Book of "L" or the Law of Maat, the goddess of equilibration. Her Venusian harmonising scales are a symbol of the balance of forces required to survive the Ordeal x or Last Judgement. The Great Work rests upon polarity. Creation comes about by division, the *Solve* of the alchemists; the Immortal Stone is attained by transcending the duality of creation through the synergetic interaction of opposites. This constitutes the remedial *Coagula* of the alchemists.

The Thelemite must integrate and unite the opposite forces under the direction of the Solar-Hermetic Lucifer or Holy Guardian Angel. The oppositions to be mastered range from *pranayama* or yogic breath control, to the ultimate unification of the personal will and True Will. The attainment of Nuit implies the achievement of her opposite, Hadit, so in the precessional Age of Aquarius the Great Work necessitates working with the magical power of Leo the Lion (or Beast), the sign opposite Aquarius on the zodiacal wheel. As Aquarius rules over the northern heaven of the Aquarian age, Leo rules over its underworld or South Pole. Gathering the Occult Force or *Kundalini* and projecting it towards Nuit or Aquarius requires the liberation of the energies of Hadit through the magick of Leo, the Beast. Union with Nuit is then possible via the portal of the non-sephira called Da'ath. Initiates of the Aeon of Hrumachis (Horus-Maat) make it their task to contact and understand the Saturnian consciousness of the Aeon. They are thus able to transcend the duality of matter and spirit for the awakening of a star within the *Khu* of an Aeon outside of time.[77]

---

[76] Ra Hoor, Heru-Khuti or "Red Horus" are Egyptian names for Mars.

[77] Saturn rules Aquarius as well as Capricorn. In the Zodiac, Aquarius and Capricorn form a dark Crater Cup for the birth of the light. The light Crater Cup is opposite, formed by Leo and Cancer, ruled by the Sun and Moon. These represent the Beast and Scarlet Woman in the world of duality. The luminary Crater Cup corresponds to the maximum expression of visible light while the Saturnian Crater Cup represents the point of maximum darkness. See *The Bacchic Mysteries*, translated by G. R. S. Mead.

Hrumachis and the Age of Aquarius

Heru-khuti, "Horus of the two horizons", was known as Harmachis to the Greeks. Heru-khuti is another name for Ra Hoor Khuit as he is named in Liber AL vel Legis. The most famous monument of Heru-khuti is the Sphinx near the Pyramids of Giza. In nearby Aunnu (Heliopolis), Heru-khuti was identified with Ra, Tum, Khephra and Hathoor—the other gods mentioned in Liber AL vel Legis. These are also indicative of the Sphinx in fourfold aspect.

Why then does the book (Liber AL vel Legis, III: 34) indicate that blessing will no longer be poured to Ra Hoor Khuit when Hrumachis arises—since both are names of Horus? Aleister Crowley thought this indicated a future Aeon of Maat. There is an affinity between Liber AL vel Legis and the Qabalah—for instance, the mantram "Aum Ha" on the last page of the book is thereby equal to the number 666.[78] The name Hrumachis might have been used for specific Qabalistic reasons. There is clearly a difference between the reign of Horus on earth—during which time blessing or "blood" is poured to him—and an event to come to pass where Horus *ascends*. In his ascent, Horus is "made Maat", his word is perfected and he comes of age. Liber AL vel Legis prophesied that Horus would be transformed into the polymorphous god represented by the Sphinx, to supersede Horus, "the Hawk headed mystical Lord". Since Hrumachis is double wanded he has been justified by Maat; the Aeon of Horus has been transformed into the double Aeon of Horus-Maat or Hrumachis.

The Initiation of Hrumachis or the New Aeon occurs fully when Maat, wielding the Sword of Zain "the doubler", cleaves the *Ka*, the soul's invisible counterpart, in two. This releases the *Ka* from the *Khaibet*, the shell or dark sphere of unconscious matter, and enables it to become self-polarised.[79]

---

[78] AUM = 111 (1 + 70 + 40); HA = 6 (5 + 1); 111 x 6 = 666.

[79] The *Thoth* Tarot depicts Horus in dual form in *The Aeon XX*. The trump corresponds Qabalistically to the letter shin, and the elements of Fire and Spirit. Shin is etymologically linked to the Egyptian word shen, whose hieroglyph is the *ankh* without the downward extension into matter—the disembodied Spirit. Aquarius corresponds to elemental Air and is part of the astrological triplicity of Air signs: Aquarius (fixed), Gemini (mutable) and Libra (cardinal). The letter for path 17 on the Tree of Life is Zain, "a sword", corresponding to Gemini. The image is Tarot Atu VI, *The Lovers*. The Sword or Lightning Flash as depicted in the symbolism of the Qabalah may represent the downward striking action of *Kundalini*—the Serpent Power or Occult Force.

The capital letters THL can be extracted from the line, "**T**o the **H**awk-headed mystical **L**ord!" By Qabalistic *Gematria* these letters are equal to: TLH "a ram", and LHT "flame", revealing the qualities of the Aeon of Horus in which blood and fire are offered as sacrifices. THL has the value of 44, a number of Horus as given in the book, and also "blood". The Ram is the symbol of Aries (♈), the sign that the Sun enters each spring equinox and whose attribution is cardinal Fire. The Energy or "blood" of the sign, and of the awakening of any aeon, is that of Mars or Horus in his martial aspect. Aquarius on the ascendant of the nativity horoscope for the age means that Scorpio is at the zenith, Taurus is at the nadir, and Leo is on the descendant. These are the four fixed signs of the Zodiac, attributed to the Sphinx. During the previous age of Pisces that began approximately 2000 years ago, the angles of the horoscope were in the mutable signs of Pisces, Virgo, Sagittarius and Gemini.[80]

By Greek Qabalah, Hrumachis adds to 779 the number of *arretos*, "unspoken". This word has several other meanings including "unknown", "secret or holy", and "abominable." The control of words and images and their transmission to mass populations became essential to those seeking power during the ideological conflicts of the 20th century. Humanity is now to be exposed, albeit subconsciously, to the disturbing knowledge that truth shall no longer be expressed in written down or spoken words.[81] According to Liber AL vel Legis, II: 22:

The exposure of innocence is a lie.

The word of truth or Maat shall now be "unspoken", for as it is cryptically put in Liber AL vel Legis, I: 10:

Let my servants be few & secret: they shall rule the many & the known.

---

[80] The age of Pisces corresponds to the rise and fall *in consciousness* of the world religions. The ultimate ideal of these has been one of unification—an ideal that is inevitably divisive in effect.

[81] The subconscious is identical to the underworld as depicted in earlier systems of thought than ours. It is the region where magick takes place, and is symbolised on the walls of the pyramids and tombs as a five-pointed star of Nuit, within a circle. When the star is depicted without a circle, it symbolises a transcendent realm of consciousness.

The condition of the people or "slaves of because" is an abomination since doctrinal enslavement leads to the actual torment of incoherence and dispersion of will—ultimately, to exhaustion of all energy and death as finality (Liber AL vel Legis, II: 27–33 and 54; III: 19). In the previous aeon, the mutability of the force called Leviathan or the Beast could be fixed to the cross of time through obedience and faith to the letter of the law. This is no longer possible since the lie or curse implicit in all written down words of truth is being made known—even if this is but dimly perceived. Lurking in the subconscious dream world of all is the abominable truth that cannot be spoken.[82]

The number 779 is also that of "Kamephis", the Black Snake, linked to *ophis* the serpent and the eye of beholding. The *ajna chakra* or third eye corresponds to Chokmah on the Tree of Life, whose number is 2 or Beth, the Magus of Tarot that creates worlds through duality. When the Serpent Power passes through the aperture of Da'ath and opens the Eye of Shiva (*ajna*)—when the eye and the serpent are one—the objective universe is no more. Duality is abolished; Reality or Gnosis is "that which remains" (Liber AL vel Legis, II: 9).

The factor of 779 is 19. When divided by 19, Hrumachis yields 41, the number of "on high", "forgetfulness" and "to the sea". Hrumachis has arisen in silence as the enigmatic Sphinx. In time there is forgetfulness of the Word that orders and harmonises cosmos. When man is the sole minister and governor of his destiny his soul is thrown to the sea, to be tossed upon the secret crest of the Beast of Chaos. When Eve, whose name has the value of 19 (ChVH), is wedded to the Beast by *love under will* then she is raised to Binah as Cosmos, by which all worlds below are ordered.

Adding the letters of HRVMAChIS by corresponding Tarot trumps produces 83.[83] According to Aleister Crowley, 83 is the number of "Consecration: love in its highest form: energy, freedom, amrita, aspiration. The root of the idea of romance plus religion."[84] Crowley's enthusiasm for the number was no doubt fuelled by its concentration into 11 (8 + 3), a number of Nuit "as all their numbers who are of us" (Liber AL vel Legis, I: 60). In a Rosicrucian magical Order, the grade of $8° = 3^{\square}$ corresponds to Binah ("Understanding"), whose virtue is Silence.

---

[82] Note that "abominable" is derived from *ab homine*, "inhuman, beastly".
[83] *The Star* (17), *The Sun* (19), *The Hierophant* (5), *The Hanged Man* (12), *The Fool* (0), *The Chariot* (VII), *The Hermit* (9) and *Art* (14) = 83.
[84] See Aleister Crowley, *Liber 777*.

Initiation

Over thousands of years the ancient Egyptians developed complex doctrines concerning the various vehicles of the human soul and spirit, and their counterparts in the macrocosm. Developing a coherent system of symbols by which knowledge of the invisible worlds may be communicated is a vital part of the Great Work and a labour of love.

The difficulty in using the Egyptian symbolism is that each *Nome* centre—an earth location for a *Neter* or god acting through nature—had its own school of metaphysics. The more complex metaphysics, however, belonged to the outer, not the inner court. In Liber AL vel Legis only the principles known as the *Khabs*, the *Khu*, and the *Ka* are mentioned directly. These are respectively the Star or Holy Guardian Angel (*Khabs*), the Magical Body (*Khu*) and the Astral Double (*Ka*). There is a fourth principle implied, as the nature of the *Ka* is dual: the *Khaibet* or Shadow.

I. The Egyptian word-symbol of the *Ka* is two upraised hands and arms. Its nature is double and is typified by the deities Horus and Set. In the non-initiate, the double *Ka* is housed—or imprisoned—by its feminine counterpart, the *Khaibet*, which is depicted hieroglyphically as a shadow form of the person.

Any man or woman has a *Ka* and a *Khaibet*, but without magical and yogic polarisation the *Ka* serves only the desire-impulses arising from the Shadow. The Shadow or *Khaibet* is bound up with the human identity or ego—which is that part of the shadow we normally think of as being "ourselves". The *Ka* double cannot then achieve its spiritual purpose by offering its substance to the Holy Guardian Angel or *Khabs* so that it may be transmuted into a *Khu* body around that Star. Only in this way is the Star alchemically "fixed", and therefore identical to that which is called the Immortal Stone of the wise.

Once Initiation has truly taken place, the *Khaibet*, which has no essential reality or substance, drops away like a shell (*qlipha*) or husk. The liberated dual principles personified as Horus and Set then divide by the power of the sword, or anti-word, of Zain. Through this polarity, Hadit causes the flame of life to arise from the womb or tomb of matter and carry his seed or *bindu* towards his Nuit or infinite bliss.

The magick of being "torn upon wheels" (Liber AL vel Legis, III: 55), the breaking of the *Khaibet*, is described in Liber AL vel Legis III, 25–29 as the swelling of Eucharistic bread or cakes of light. The Initiate experiences this through the ophidian vibrations of the rising *Kundalini* or Serpent Power and the resulting phenomena—or emission of beetles, as it is described in the book.

II. The *Ka* in the normal state of affairs is a mass of appetites and desires that ultimately lead to dispersion and spiritual death. It seems that one can only either satisfy these desires—which is impossible, since their source is groundless—or attempt to keep them under control by suppressing them. It is clear that no attempt to suppress the appetites of the human *Ka* by the way of moral, religious, or other rules of conduct has ever actually worked. Control can be enforced through severities, but the very severities then replace the appetites. Thus, throughout the long, dark history of humanity, man has been his own jailer, torturer, and executioner.

III. There is a way out of this called Initiation. Every truly initiatory path requires the highest standards of training and discipline. A person must pass through trial and ordeal; there is a Great Work to be done. To begin with, such trials are not spiritual ones and consist merely of opposition from within the person themselves. However, unless the opposition within the self is mastered *by the aspirant*, no progress is made. In the majority of cases this threshold is never passed at all, for the appetites of the *Ka* are overwhelming and take on countless guises. The successful aspirant, on the other hand, strengthens the *Ka* spiritually through redirecting its hunger and thirst towards spiritual knowledge. In this way, the spiritual will is strengthened and the power of the shadow to absorb all the energy of the self is weakened.

Patanjali's *Eight Limbs of Yoga* is a fair representation of the initial training of the *Ka*. This includes self-study, reading of scriptures, fiery aspiration and self-surrender among the actions to be taken. There are also various abstentions. These need not be thought of as *moral* abstentions. The word of Sin is Restriction. The Initiate has a predisposition towards wilfully imposing such limits or abstentions that will lead to his or her liberation. The Great Work is not for those who are weak-minded or that lack the ability to practise the discrimination that is essential on the path of Knowledge.

The Eight Limbs of Yoga (Patanjali)

(i)   *Yamas* (abstentions): Harmlessness; truthfulness; non-stealing; continence; non-covetousness

(ii)   *Niyamas* (observances): Cleanliness; contentment; fiery aspiration; self-study; self-surrender (to the path)

(iii)   *Asana* (seated posture)

(iv)   *Pranayama* (control of breath)

(v)   *Pratyahara* (withdrawal of senses)

(vi)   *Dharana* (concentration, fixation)

(vii)   *Dhyana* (sustained concentration)

(viii) *Samadhi* (transcendence, union with God)

One should meditate on the meaning of these as practical considerations. "Harmlessness" for example, is to refrain from doing and thinking all that would involve the energy of the self in the endless repercussions, justifications and conciliations that are the ordinary consequences of doing harm to another being. Most of the abstentions are about conserving the energy of the seer or yogi to the Great Work. "Truthfulness" can mean, ultimately, doing and even *thinking* only that which is true, or the True Will.

IV. The *Ka,* at a further stage, is directed upwardly by the will. This can only take place once the dual *Ka* twins have been released from the *Khaibet.* In all traditions that have developed practical means for attainment, a symbol variously described as a body of light, chariot, vehicle, or even space capsule, is constructed by intelligent use of the will and imagination. The heart or centre of the body that has been identified with such a mandala may variously be termed as a pyramid, mountain, cave or labyrinth. The *Ka* then inhabits a Great Symbol of the Universe.

According to various traditions, the Great Symbol is poetically named Jerusalem, Abiegnus, Zion, Babylon, Adam-Kadmon, Sphinx, Phoenix, Ab-Hati, Duat, On (Heliopolis), or Nile. The notions of God, City and Man are combined in one symbol. The symbol or mandala is built over a lengthy period of time and with detailed and painstaking care; ultimately consciousness must expand in the six directions of space: North and South, East and West, Above and Below.

V. The *Ka* can now be strengthened by various ways and means in its upward tending path. It is fed on *nectar* or ambrosia of the Gods, as are the members of a spiritual Order (whether incarnate or discarnate) once the *Ka* has been bound in service. The shadow, *Khaibet*, has all the while been broken down, dissolved, and reformed in the Averse image of a God. It then rules over the hell world of demons as a Guardian.

VI. The consciousness transferred to the *Ka* is seated in a chariot by which it is able to travel to places otherwise inaccessible to the human mind. The *Ka* now obeys the conscious will like a trained animal and takes pleasure in the exercise. It has lost its taste for the illusionary or "weak" pleasures that captivate the earthbound soul. Gradually, delights of a wholly different nature begin to become apparent via new, non-material and extremely subtle senses that the *Ka* has begun to realise.

VII. The *Ka* of an Initiate is double when it is fully polarised. The flame of Spirit-Fire, the *Zel* (ZL, 37), has been awakened. This spirit-flame or seed of stars seeks its return through the veil of time and space to its source, its originality. The double at this stage can be realised, since it is fully polarised, as an earthly and a celestial *Ka*. The celestial aspect of the *Ka* is the *Khu*. The *Ka* and *Khu* are as the twin gods Horus and Set who preside over Initiation. As Zain, Gemini, they are the breath of spirit entering and leaving the nostrils of Ra, fluctuating in cosmic tides.

VIII. The world of the *Ka* equates to that of Yetzirah in the Qabalah, while that of the *Khu* equates to the world of Briah, above the Abyss. The transformation of the *Ka* into a *Khu* establishes the birth of water mentioned in the Gospel of St. John (3: 1–21). The ordeals of Initiation are described in Liber AL vel Legis, III: 63–67:

63.   The fool readeth this Book of the Law, and its comment; & he understandeth it not.

64.   Let him come through the first ordeal, & it will be to him as silver.

65.   Through the second, gold.

66.   Through the third, stones of precious water.

67.   Through the fourth, ultimate sparks of the intimate fire.

"The fool" of verse 63 is one that has not yet begun the path of Initiation. The ordeals of Set and Horus are described as silver and gold in verses 64 and 65. The elemental temptation of Set is to stay in a world of astral glamour and illusion; the spiritual temptation of Horus is to rule over the world using magical powers that correspond to Yetzirah, the Astral Plane.

The angels of Yetzirah, whose heavily seductive realm must be passed through on the way to the celestial *Khu*, are also devils or fallen angels, as are all those that minister to man and his *Ka*. Lucifer is the archetypal fallen angel and the prototype of the Holy Guardian Angel. According to legend he is the Teacher of Humanity. His teaching brings liberation to some, while for others the reward is slavery and destruction. All this is typical of the intensely dualistic world of Ruach, the mind or Spirit, and of Yetzirah, the Astral Plane.

When the ordeals of silver and gold have been successfully passed, there follows the birth or baptism of the celestial *Khu*, described in verse 66 as "stones of precious water". The astral body is discarded and the consciousness of the Adept fully enters the spiritual plane. The water of Briah is that shown surrounding the god Amoun on Egyptian papyri, the Hidden God who comes forth in Silence. The accomplishment of the first three ordeals will automatically lead the Adept to the supreme transcendence described in verse 67, the "ultimate sparks of the intimate fire."

IX. A crossroads of the soul is arrived at with each ordeal. To master the Astral Plane, the Adept must learn to deal with and transcend intense realisations of good and evil, so-called. In spite of the atmosphere of truth, holy awe and religious devotion that may very well accompany such realisations, none of them are in fact true; certainly they are not what the Eastern sages refer to as "Reality".[85]

---

[85] The reader is referred to the writings of Swami Vivekananda.

Any dualistic phenomenon is a product of mind, and the mind's first encounter with that which is beyond it. Here is the primary temptation as typified by the legend of Christ and Satan in the wilderness. The 40 days Christ spent there corresponds Qabalistically to the Hebrew letter Mem, which means, "water". The word-symbol for this letter is *The Hanged Man* of Tarot, showing forth in detail the nature of this Initiation. The Adept must become the master of time and space, and enter the Hermetic Plane—the realm of pure mind. The Adept portrayed in Atu XII has not been hanged as such, but is rather suspended *upside-down* between the worlds; he is neither fully in the world of spirit, nor is he fully immersed in the waters 'below', the Astral Plane, which he knows by now to be a deception.

We differ here from the view of Aleister Crowley who, in *The Book of Thoth,* indicated that the mystery of *The Hanged Man XII* pertains only to a bygone age called the "Aeon of Osiris". Even Crowley's own Tarot trump design did not depict Osiris, but Typhon the Destroyer in a reversed posture.[86] The meaning of this image goes beyond the mere cyclical or seasonal recurrence of vegetable life that is frequently put forward as an explanation for perplexing chthonic items dug up from the past.[87]

The purpose of the Great Work as expressed in the language of alchemy is to give birth to an Immortal Stone. This is an Individuality that is both one and none as it is made of two coexistent but un-manifested principles:

The Perfect and the Perfect are one Perfect and not two; nay, they are none!

Liber AL vel Legis, I: 45

---

[86] Aleister Crowley intended to depict Osiris by the crown worn by the skeletal figure in his Tarot card for *Death XIII*. The posture of *The Hanged Man XII* depicts the symbol of the Spiritual Sun rising above the Waters of Space—the triangle surmounted by a cross or "Golden Dawn". Crowley's Osirian description of *The Hanged Man* in *The Book of Thoth* is at odds with his practical use of the card's symbolism, where he identified it with the ritual magick and yogic practices he recommended for use in his Order of A∴ A∴ See Crowley's *Liber Pyramidos*, a ritual he designed for his own use when he wished to attain the grade of Magister Templi, and later, as a ritual for Neophytes.

[87] Any anthropomorphic god is invariably described as a "fertility god"!

Once duality is abolished, so is the possibility of anything finite, as the finite only exists by virtue of its opposite. Therefore the reality that is veiled by the metaphor of the star or *Khabs* is not limited:

Every number is infinite; there is no difference.

Liber AL vel Legis, I: 4

X. If it is the Will of the Angel, then he unites with the *Ka* double by assuming the substance of the *Ka* and transmuting it into his own body, the *Khu*. The waters of space are moved by this magick; for the Adeptus Minor there is a trauma on all the planes, a 'shockwave' or 'earthquake'. In uniting with the *Ka*, the Angel recollects his own fall from heaven.[88] The "fall" was the birth of the Angel along with all other primal or chaos gods. These are the children of the Beast, or Chokmah considered as the Atziluthic world that the Beast begets upon the Scarlet Woman or Binah. The recollection or remembrance of the Angel or *Khabs* is then communicated to the *Khu* and thereby to the human soul—which the *Khabs*, by this time, informs. As the Angel's seed of light is fused with the egg of the human soul via its *Khu*, the Will current descends along the 13th path of *The Priestess of the Silver Star*.

To bring the Knowledge and Conversation of the Holy Guardian Angel to perfection, the *Ka* must realise itself through dissolution into the heavenly *Khu*, the Qabalistic world of Briah. Both man and Angel partake of this, but it signals the annihilation of the man (or ego). The Angel returns across the Abyss with the soul, for these are two and none. The man no longer is.

XI. The ultimate transcendence is referred to in the Egyptian Book of the Law, Liber AL vel Legis, III: 67: "Through the fourth [ordeal], ultimate sparks of the intimate fire."

XII. Who accomplishes this is "chosen" of Nuit. They may then manifest the Holy Guardian Angel even while living in a body of flesh, upon the earth.

---

[88] This should not be confused with a fall from grace.

Epilogue

The Law is for all. There is nothing to be gained by looking for psychological or other remedies that require, and search for, a cause within the human personality itself. The pursuit of objects to cleave to the self is the root of all that afflicts the human soul, since it results in the word of Sin that is the Restriction of the True Will:

The word of Sin is Restriction.

Liber AL vel Legis, I: 41

There is, however, a hidden assistant, a secret means. Such a means is secreted within the nature of love herself, which is the desire to unite with that outside or beyond the self. When the desire to unite, no matter what, is transferred to the love of wisdom and the wisdom seed, then the desire of the *Ka*, the magick wand of the magician, is brought to the Great Work, the magical cup or Holy Graal. And therein is the fulfilment of the Hermetic Arcanum.

Appendices

The Master Key of Thelemic Atomic Correspondences

Thelema and Hermetic Qabalah	Atomic Theory and Biochemistry
Hadit	The electron (-1), the magnet The symbol of the electron as magnet is Iron, whose atomic number is 26, Ayin ע and the number of the Middle Pillar, through which the electromagnetic power of Hadit (or 93 current) passes through creation
And out of his mouth goeth a sharp sword, that with it he should smite the nations: and he shall rule them with a rod of iron. (Revelation, 19: 15)	
The Body of Nuit or Scarlet Woman	The electron cloud; the quantum field; the *Khu* or unfragmented body
And the sign shall be my ecstasy, the consciousness of the continuity of existence, the unfragmentary non-atomic fact of my universality. (Liber AL vel Legis, I: 26, holograph manuscript)	
I do set my bow in the cloud, and it shall be for a token of a covenant between me and the earth. (Genesis, 9: 13)	
Behold, the glory of the Lord appeared in the cloud. (Exodus, 16: 10)	
The Beast or *Khabs*, Atziluth above and Yetzirah below	The proton (+1)
The Scarlet Woman, *Khu* or Briah above, the *Ka* or Assiah below	The neutron, neutral (0), transformed into an electron and a proton (2) when activated by electromagnetism
Heru-ra-ha	The quark. Each proton and neutron contains 3 quarks (3=1), of which there are two kinds:
Hoor-paar-kraat and Ra Hoor Khuit	The down quark and the up quark
The universe above the Abyss	The quantum field or electron cloud
The universe below the Abyss	The atom nucleus, made up of proton and neutron
Path of Aleph, Tarot Atu 0 *The Fool*	Hydrogen, atomic number 1, made of 1 electron and 1 proton (no neutron) Hydrogen can also be attributed to Chokmah or Atziluth, the *Khabs* or Beast

Path of Beth, Tarot Atu I *The Magus*	Helium, atomic number 2, made of 2 electrons, 2 protons and 2 neutrons; helium is the first element to contain neutrons; helium can also be attributed to Binah or Briah, the *Khu* or Scarlet Woman
Da'ath and the formation of the Ruach	Oxygen, atomic number 8
The Sphinx as 666, Tiphereth	Carbon, atomic number 6, containing 6 electrons, 6 protons, and 6 neutrons
Hydrogen atoms first fuse together into a helium atom then helium fuses into carbon; carbon atoms (the Sun/Son) can then fuse with helium (the Mother) into oxygen (Da'ath, Knowledge)	
The Zodiac and Precession of the Equinoxes	The carbon cycle; diamond formation
The Strong Nuclear Force	The True Will
The Weak Nuclear Force	The personal will
The altar of brass and Liber AL vel Legis, III: 30	The atom nucleus or world below the Abyss symbolised by brass, an alloy of copper and zinc; the atomic number of copper is 30, the path of Resh, the Sun; the atomic number of zinc is 29, the path of Qoph, the Moon; copper represents the proton, *Khabs*, Yetzirah, the Beast or Holy Guardian Angel; zinc represents the neutron, the *Ka*, and Assiah; copper and zinc must be 'raised' as gold and silver, whose atomic numbers are 79 and 47; by addition, 79 + 47 = 126, the number of On or Aunnu, the "City of the Sun" and birthplace of Horus; this is achieved through self-polarisation, whereby the neutral *Ka* (0) becomes active as 2
Moreover he made an altar of brass, twenty cubits the length thereof, and twenty cubits the breadth thereof, and ten cubits the height thereof. (2 Chronicles, 4: 1)	
My Altar is of open brass work; burn thereon in silver or gold! (Liber AL vel Legis, III: 30)	

The Hermetic Tree of Life: Principal Correspondences

Tarot	Title	Letter	Value	Attribute		English	Path
0	*The Fool*	Aleph	1	△		Ox (Plough)	11
I	*The Magus*	Beth	2	☿		House	12
II	*The Priestess*	Gimel	3	☽		Camel	13
III	*The Empress*	Daleth	4	♀		Door	14
IV	*The Emperor*	Tzaddi	90	♈		Fishhook	28
V	*The Hierophant*	Vav	6	♉		Nail, pin	16
VI	*The Lovers*	Zain	7	♊		Sword	17
VII	*The Chariot*	Cheth	8	♋		Fence	18
VIII	*Adjustment*	Lamed	30	♎		Ox goad	22
IX	*The Hermit*	Yod	10	♍		Hand	20
X	*Fortune*	Kaph	20	♃		Palm (of the hand)	21
XI	*Lust*	Teth	9	♌		Snake	19
XII	*The Hanged Man*	Mem	40	▽		Water	23
XIII	*Death*	Nun	50	♏		Fish	24
XIV	*Art*	Samekh	60	♐		Prop, support	25
XV	*The Devil*	Ayin	70	♑		Eye	26
XVI	*The Tower*	Pé	80	♂		Mouth	27
XVII	*The Star*	Ilé	5	♒		Window	15
XVIII	*The Moon*	Qoph	100	♓		Back of the head	29
XIX	*The Sun*	Resh	200	☉		Head	30
XX	*The Aeon*	Shin	300	⊕	△	Tooth	31
XXI	*The Universe*	Tav	400	♄	▽	Egyptian Tau	32

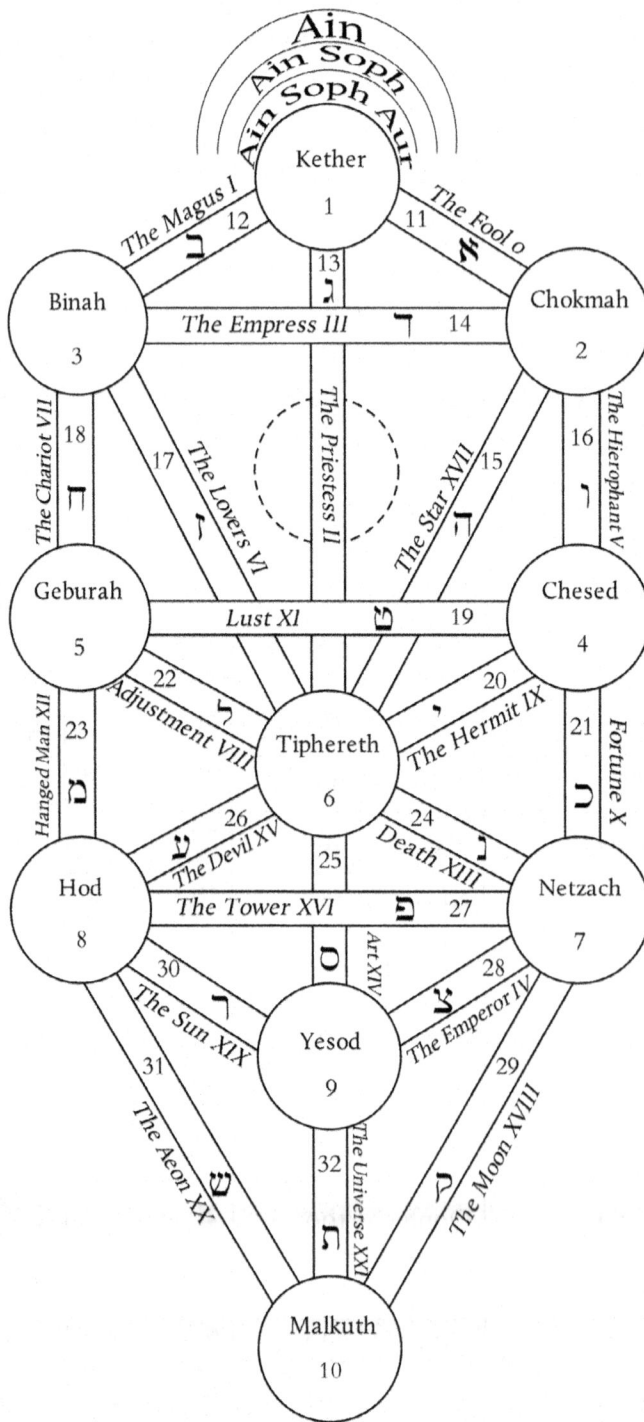

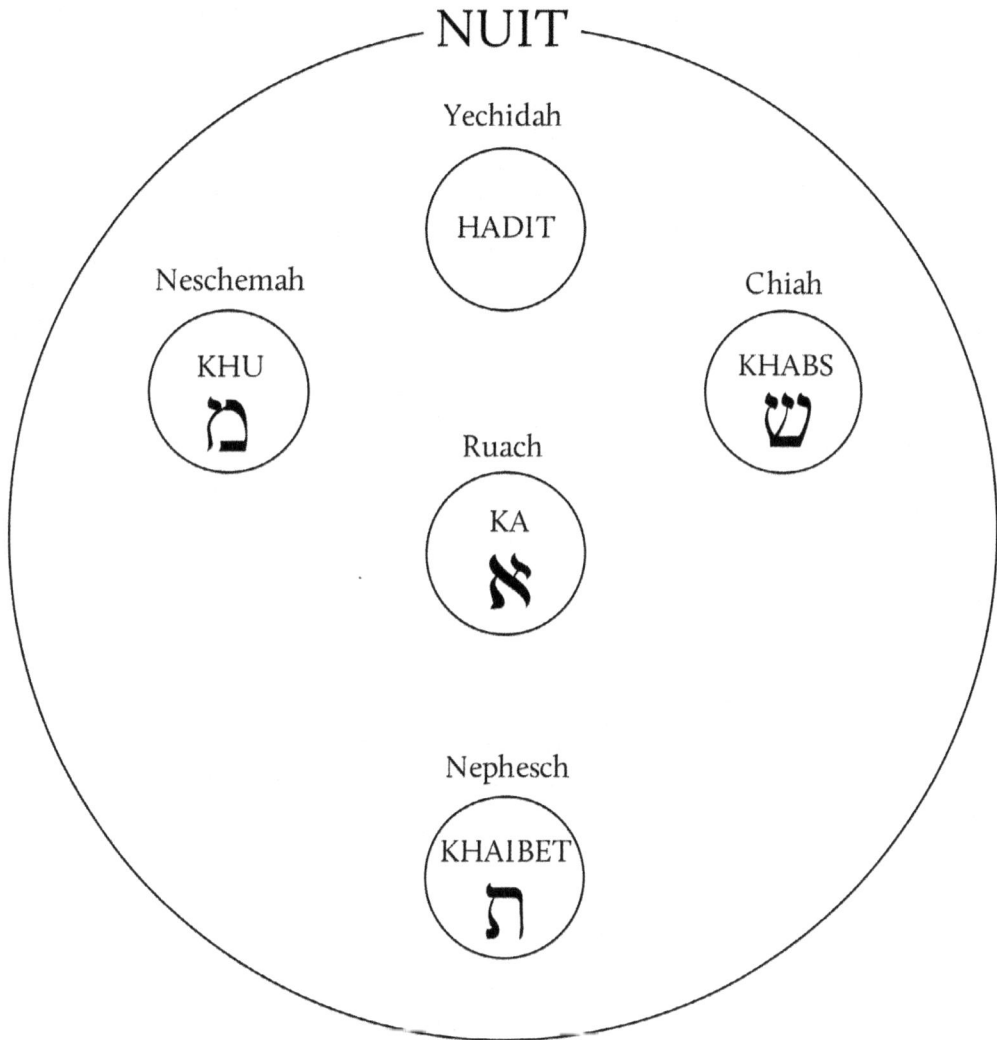

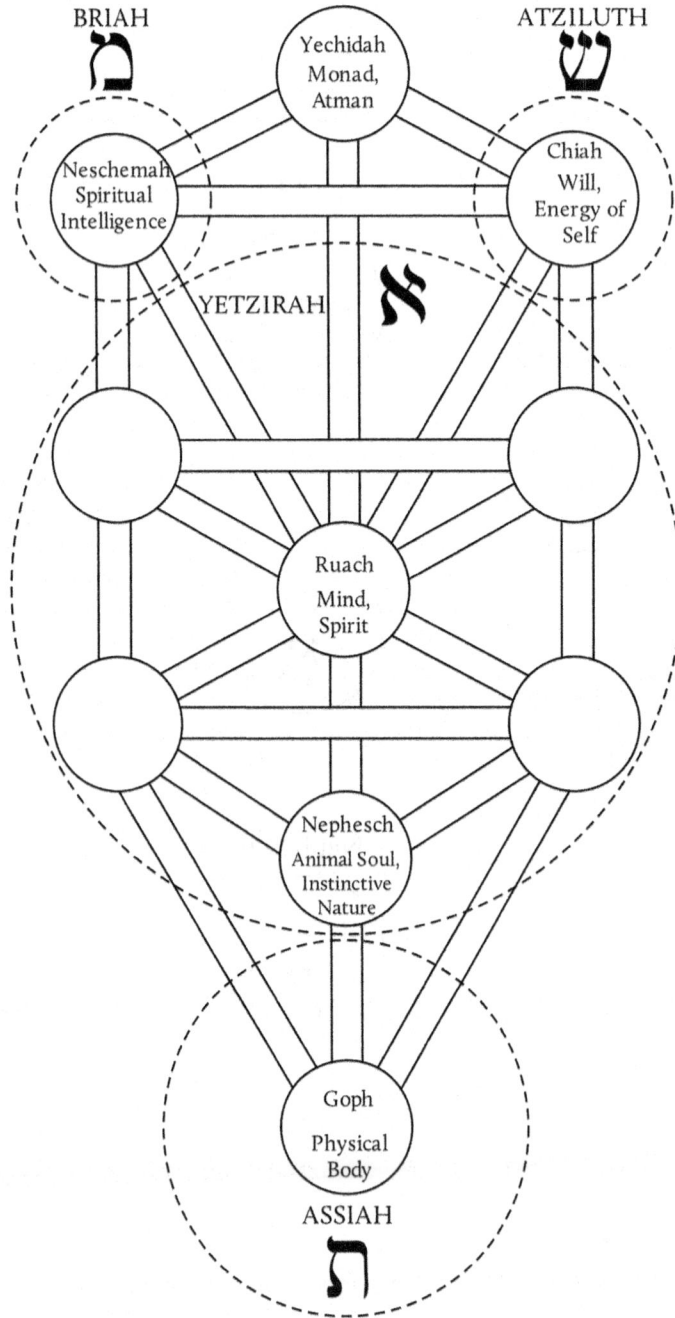

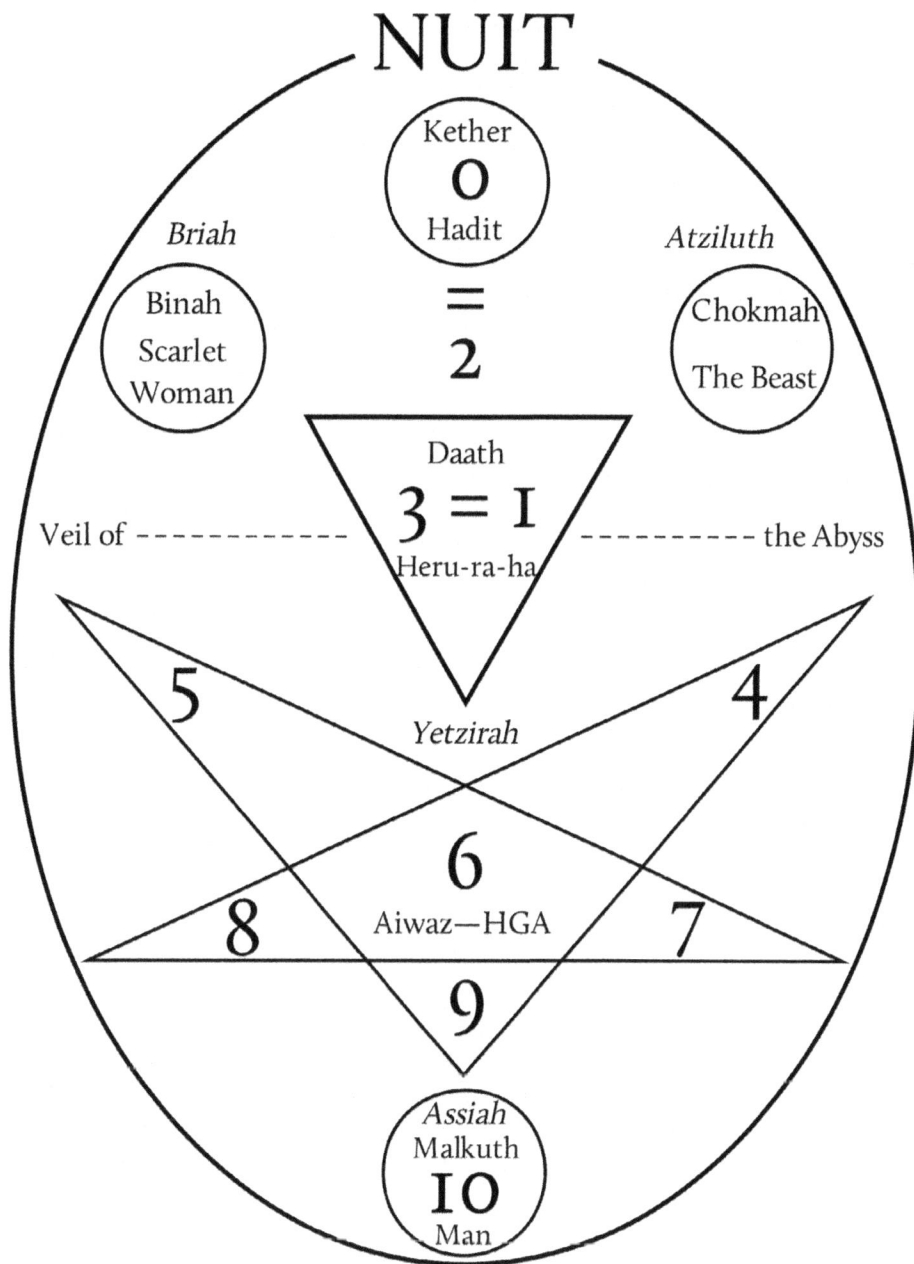

The Tree of L or MAAT

Above the Abyss: $0° = 2^□$ and the Supernal Field of L or MAAT, whose Symbol is the Ankh of Life.

The Thelemic formula of the Supernals is $0° = 2^□$. The "zero" here expresses an individual centre of consciousness or Hadit, who is un-manifested and un-extended. It is therefore an Individuality that is perfect and complete and which, as such, is *Not*:

For I am perfect, being Not ... I am none indeed.

Liber AL vel Legis, II: 15

The manifestation of this perfect unit of consciousness requires that it divides itself into two interactive principles: the Scarlet Woman and the Beast, a body and its head; a *Khu* and a *Khabs,* a universe and a word or True Will to order it and give it form. Above the Abyss the two principles coexist in perfect union and harmony. They are as yet un-manifested; they are none, and therefore equal to Hadit himself, for:

The Perfect and the Perfect are one Perfect and not two; nay, they are none!

Liber AL vel Legis, I: 45

On the Tree of Life, the Beast and the Scarlet Woman correspond to the spheres of Chokmah and Binah, Will and Understanding. When the Four Worlds of the Qabalah are represented on the Tree, the "two" are the worlds of Atziluth and Briah.[89] Atziluth is the world of pure Will, the Word, and the Beast. Briah is the creative world, the body of Nuit, the world of Love and Understanding, the Scarlet Woman. By reverse correspondence, the formula of $0° = 2^□$ is an expression of 20, Kaph, the Wheel which generates the first motion towards manifestation. It is the fountain of life pouring forth the 93 current of love under will.

---

[89] When the Four Worlds are represented on one Tree of Life then the Tree becomes a symbol of the Qabalistic formula of Tetragrammaton (ShMATh) —and therefore of the cosmos.

The Abyss: $3^\circ = 1^\square$

The Abyss is the projection of 3, the result of 2 united in a third, and is the Knowledge that begets world appearance or cosmos. The $3^\circ = 1^\square$ formula describes the unity of the first descending triad, Chokmah, Binah and Da'ath (ChKMH BINH VDOTh), the number of which is 620. This is also the number of Kether (KThR) the Crown, to which they give expression. On the Tree of L the position of Kether is attributed to Hadit; the first descending triad manifests the consciousness of Hadit, who is the "Knower" and the giver of Life.

The formula of $3^\circ = 1^\square$ corresponds to the number 13 as equal to Achad (AChD), "one". The individual unit of consciousness is manifested by the interaction of two opposite principles that mutually define one another.[90] Individual consciousness is dualistic, as "one" can only exist in contrast to "not one", or that which it is *not.* The double god Heru-ra-ha manifests this duality, whose twin aspects are Hoor-paar-kraat, silent and withdrawn as the Babe of the Abyss, and Ra Hoor Khuit, projected as the Holy Spirit uttering the Word of the Aeon to the Holy Guardian Angel in Yetzirah. As the Astral Light of individual consciousness, Heru Ra Ha is the Son of the Supernal $0^\circ = 2^\square$. He is the turning point or field of operation between Nuit as Maat above the Abyss, and her Word manifested below the Abyss by Ra Hoor Khuit.

The formula of $3^\circ = 1^\square$ corresponds to 31, the number of the path of Shin, the triple tongue of the Holy Spirit. As 31, the spirit fire of Ra Hoor Khuit is equal to 620 divided by 20: the Wheel of $2^\circ = 0^\square$ pouring forth the 93 current. Through the turning point of Da'ath, "two" is no longer equal to 0 but becomes equal to 7, the number of creation.[91] The number 7 is that of the letter Zain, the Flaming Sword ruling over the (seven) sephiroth below the Abyss.

Below the Abyss: $7^\circ = 2^\square$ and the World of Duality, ZAIN

The formula is now $7^\circ = 2^\square$ the Sword of Zain. The "two" are manifested below the Abyss as the polarity between the Scarlet Woman, man's natural soul, and the Beast her Holy Guardian Angel.

---

[90] The number 13 corresponds Qabalistically to the word AChD, "Unity".

[91] In the book of Genesis, God creates the world in seven days. Seven is also the number of the sphere of Netzach ruled by Venus whose symbol is the Ankh of Life. In the Tarot, Atu VII *The Chariot* represents the magical body or *Khu* containing creation.

The interaction of these two is love, 7, a number of Venus. By correspondence to the Four Worlds of the Qabalah, the Scarlet Woman is Assiah while the Beast is Yetzirah. Between them are born the seven sub-abysmal spheres of the Tree of Life. The Tree of Life below the Abyss (worlds of Yetzirah and Assiah) springs from the consciousness of Hadit working through:

1. The Beast and Scarlet Woman above the Abyss.

2. Heru-ra-ha, the manifested individual consciousness emerging from the Abyss as a consequence of the interaction of the Beast and Scarlet Woman. The nature of this manifested unit of individual consciousness is dual, comprising of the opposite principles of the Beast and Scarlet Woman. These two are the spirit or Holy Guardian Angel and man's natural soul, respectively attributed to the Qabalistic Worlds of Yetzirah and Assiah.

3. Ra Hoor Khuit, the projected aspect of Heru-ra-ha. Ra Hoor Khuit utters the Word to the Holy Guardian Angel in Yetzirah.

The Universe

The consciousness of Hadit reaches the material world through man's natural soul, the Scarlet Woman, who receives this consciousness current from the Holy Guardian Angel or Beast in Yetzirah. The formula of $7^{\circ} = 2^{\square}$ corresponds to 72, the number of the OB or magical light which is Atziluth's Secret Nature. The OB is also the secret nature of the Beast, the first expression of Hadit down the planes. The seven sephiroth below the Abyss therefore manifest that light, the light of Chokmah, Wisdom, whose number is 2. Looking at the *Tree of L* in the Four Worlds, the Universe manifested through Da'ath by the consciousness of the Knower (Hadit) thus extends into the formative world of Yetzirah, the world of the Holy Guardian Angel. The Malkuth of Yetzirah is the Crown of the material world, Assiah, the world of man's natural soul. The latter is symbolised by the Scarlet Woman who is the vehicle of incarnation of the individual unit of consciousness into matter. The purpose of man's incarnation is to fully form and individualise this unit of consciousness; the aim of the Hermetic Great Work is to wholly transform it by love under will. This is accomplished through the polarisation of its twin aspects, spirit and soul, into a synergetic relationship—thus expanding the field of consciousness to an infinite degree.

Glossary

Abrahadabra

The formula of the transfiguration of man's elemental nature into a *Khu*, the Holy Graal or magical body in which Initiates are born forth to the stars of the body of Nuit. By Hebrew Qabalah the number of Abrahadabra is 418, the number of Nuit's love chant, "To Me", which indicates to the Initiate where his destination lies. Abrahadabra is "the reward of Ra Hoor Khut". The "reward" is for those who are able to pass the ordeals of Ra Hoor Khuit, the Angel of the Last Judgement. *See also Horus; Khu; Heaven, company of; Ra Hoor Khuit.*

Abyss

The chasm through which consciousness "falls" from non-duality into duality. The nature of the Abyss is mind; its function is division. Out of it emerges creation—the universe as perceived by the dualistic mind that separates forms and defines them by contrast. The division represented by the Abyss separates the Tree of Life from the Tree of the Knowledge of Good and Evil. It separates macrocosm from microcosm, heaven from earth, and eternity from perpetuity. The "crossing of the Abyss" is the Initiation that the soul must undergo to overcome world illusion. The Abyss is named Da'ath, meaning "Knowledge". Da'ath is the root of "death" which, whether actual or initiatory, is the means of crossing the Abyss. The relationship between knowledge and death is made explicit by Hadit in Liber AL vel Legis, II: 6, where he says: "I am Life, and the giver of Life, yet therefore is the knowledge of me the knowledge of death." *See also Fall; Hadit.*

Aeon (and Aeon of Horus)

The word aeon, meaning "age" in Greek, refers to an indefinite period of time, an eternity. Metaphysically, an aeon refers to a power existing outside of time. Such a power represents a particular level of consciousness. An aeon may thus be objective, in which case it corresponds to a historical age, or subjective, in which case it exists outside of time and corresponds to a magical universe. The Aeon of Horus is the eternity presided over by the god Horus (Greek) or Heru-ra-ha (Egyptian), the god of death and resurrection. *See also Horus; Heru-ra-ha; Thelema.*

Ahathoor

Egyptian goddess worshipped especially at Aunnu (Heliopolis), where she represents the aspect of Isis who gave birth to Horus. Ahathoor is also the mother of the star Sirius or Sothis. Her name literally means "House of Horus"; as his dwelling she is his *Khu*, and Horus is her *Khabs*. This identifies Horus, as *Khabs*, with the star of Set or Sept. The star represents the seventh *chakra*, which stands outside the human body. The awakening or birth of this seventh lotus is the object of the Great Work.

The Greek name of Ahathoor is Aphrodite, the goddess of love; her Roman name is Venus, and to the Greeks she was Astarte. Esoterically, the planet Venus is considered to emanate from the star Sirius—or from the point of view of earth, the celestial path of Venus crosses that of Sirius. Ahathoor is the prototype of the Scarlet Woman or soul. As the soul in the underworld, she is usually depicted wearing scarlet; in her celestial aspect she is naked and clothed with stars, thus closely identified with Nuit. *See also Aunnu; Chakra; Horus; Khabs; Khu.*

Aiwass (or Aiwaz)

The praeterhuman intelligence that transmitted Liber AL vel Legis to Aleister Crowley in Cairo in 1904 e.v. By Hebrew Qabalah, the number of Aiwaz is 93, the number of Thelema, the "word of the Law" of the Aeon of Horus given by Nuit (Liber AL vel Legis, I: 39). By Greek Qabalah, Aiwass adds up to 418, the number of the "reward" of Ra Hoor Khut, Abrahadabra. Nuit refers to Aiwass as "the minister of Hoor-paar-kraat". Hoor-paar-kraat represents the un-manifested universe. Hoor-paar-kraat is the silent, withdrawn aspect of the double god Heru-ra-ha. His twin is Ra Hoor Khuit, the manifested universe. *See also Abrahadabra; Heru-ra-ha; Holy Guardian Angel; Ra Hoor Khuit; Thelema.*

Ankh-af-na-khonsu

An Egyptian Initiatic cult name adopted by priests and scribes of Thebes. The Ankh-af-na-khonsu priest of the Stele of Revealing lived in the XXVIth Dynasty. This late Egyptian dynasty extended between the years 663 and 525 BCE, a time during which the history of Egypt became increasingly merged into that of the Middle East and Greece. The Ankh-af-na-khonsu cult flourished at the same time as that of the Old Testament prophet Ezekiel, and the reign of the Babylonian King Nebuchadnezzar described at the beginning of the book of Daniel.

106

This period of history coincides with the end of the Kingdom of Judah, which culminated with the Babylonian capture of Jerusalem and the destruction of the Temple in 587 BCE. Ezekiel predicted these events around the year 600 BCE, shortly after the deportation to Babylon, a time at which the Temple had been taken over by "pagan" cults. It is around this time also (in 622 BCE) that the priest Hilkiah (see 2 Chronicles 34: 14 or 2 Kings 22: 8) claimed to have rediscovered the Jewish Book of the Law in the Temple of Yahweh. Therefore a priest of Ankh-af-na-khonsu received the eschatological revelation recorded on his stele at a time that was very much heralding the end of an age, the end of the Kingdom of Judah. This marked the beginning of a tumultuous period that paved the way for the messianic era.

The cult name of Ankh-af-na-khonsu refers to the moon god Khonsu.[92] Khonsu, whose name means "traveller of the sky", was worshipped at Thebes as the son of Amoun and Mut. The name Ankh-af-na-khonsu literally means "Life (*ankh*) of the traveller of the sky (*khonsu*)". The Ankh-af-na-khonsu Initiate became master of the forces of the underworld, overcame death and entered the immortal realm of the Aeon of Horus. The revelation, apocalypse or words of truth are recorded on the funeral stone, the Stele of Revealing. Approximately two thousand five hundred years later, the Stele of Revealing played a central part in the transmission of Liber AL vel Legis. Ankh-af-na-khonsu Initiates are self-slain, risen masters whose secrets are revealed by Nuit to her chosen lovers. Ankh-af-na-khonsu is referred to by the gods in the book as priest of the princes, scribe, prophet, and warrior lord of Thebes. *See also Nuit; Thelema; Set; Stele of Revealing.*

Assiah

The Hebrew word for "matter", and the name given to the material world in the Qabalah. Assiah corresponds to the sphere of Malkuth on the Tree of Life, and to the final letter Hé of the classical formula of Tetragrammaton. The intelligence ruling over Assiah is the Scarlet Woman in the underworld. By Hebrew Qabalah, the number of Assiah is 385. This is also the number of Shekinah, the term used by theologians for the divine feminine presence, represented as light. The name derives from *sakan*, meaning, "to dwell, rest". *See the Scarlet Woman; Tetragrammaton; Worlds, Four.*

---

[92] By Hebrew Qabalah, Khonsu (ChNShV) adds to the number 364, a lunar number since it is that of the lunar year of 13 x 28 days.

Atom

The basic building block of matter, consisting of a dense nucleus surrounded by a cloud of electrons. The nucleus of the atom is typically composed of protons and neutrons, except in the case of the element Hydrogen, whose nucleus only consists of one proton. Nearly all the mass of the atom is contained in its nucleus, which only occupies a tiny fraction of the space inside the atom, the rest being filled by the electron cloud. Electrons and protons are electrically charged, and their respective charges are opposite to each other. The charge of the electron is negative, while that of the proton is positive. These opposite charges attract each other and act as the two poles of a magnet, their attraction creating the force that holds together the atom nucleus. The total electric charge of the atom results from the combination of the positive and negative charges of its protons and electrons. These are normally in equal proportions, the total charge of the atom being consequently neutral. The charges of the electron and proton determine their interaction with each other and with other electrically charged particles. Whereas two opposite charges attract one another, two identical charges will repel each other. *See also Atomic Bonding; Atomic Forces; Atomic Number; Electron; Magnetism; Neutron; Periodic Table of the Elements; Proton; Quantum Theory.*

Atomic Bonding

Atoms bond together to complete their valence shell. They can bond by either sharing a pair of electrons, thereby forming a covalent bond, or by losing or gaining electrons to form ionic bonds. If an atom only has a few electrons in its valence shell, its tendency will be to lose those electrons so that the next lower shell, which is full, becomes its valence shell. The reverse takes place in atoms only requiring a few more electrons to complete their valence shell. These atoms will tend to steal electrons from other atoms in order to complete their outermost layer or valence shell. Atoms bonded covalently form molecules, which can be made of anything from two to thousands of atoms. One of the elements that most readily form covalent bonds is carbon, important in the formation of organic life. When atoms bond ionically by losing or gaining electrons, their electrical charge no longer remains neutral as the number of protons and electrons in the atom are no longer equal. They acquire a net positive or negative electrical charge and are called ions. Positively charged ions are called cations, and negatively charged ones are called anions.

As a result of their opposite charges, the ions attract each other electromagnetically, forming ionic bonds. This bonding is typical of crystals, solid materials made up of alternating positive and negative ions building up in a solid lattice or framework. *See also Atom; Carbon; Electron; Neutron; Proton.*

Atomic Forces

Atoms are kept stable by the influence of three of the four fundamental forces of nature—the electromagnetic force, the strong nuclear force and the weak nuclear force. The only natural force that does not bear an impact on atomic stability is gravity, which only affects much larger objects. Atomic forces exercise a push or a pull upon the atom. The electromagnetic force holds the electron cloud around the atom nucleus; the strong nuclear force maintains the protons and neutrons together in the nucleus; the weak nuclear force exercises its influence on the process of decay that takes place in an atom nucleus containing an excess of protons or neutrons. *See also Atom; Electron; Magnetism; Neutron; Proton.*

Atomic Number

Abbreviated as "Z", the atomic number is determined by the number of protons included in an atom's nucleus. As most atoms contain an equal number of protons and electrons, this number frequently indicates the total number of electrons in the atom, the main factor influencing the atom's chemical and physical properties. *See also Atom; Electron; Proton.*

Atziluth

The Hebrew word for "emanation", and the name given to the divine or archetypal world in the Qabalah. The world of Atziluth corresponds to the sphere of Chokmah on the Tree of Life, and to the letter Yod of the classical formula of Tetragrammaton. The Intelligence ruling over the world of Atziluth is the Beast, the life-giving spirit manifested as the centre of consciousness or star called *Khabs* in Liber AL vel Legis. By Hebrew Qabalah the word Atziluth adds up to 537. This is the number of the word for "uterine aperture". Atziluth thus represents the breaking of the womb of infinity, Nuit, so that life may be emanated from it. The word emanation comes from the Latin *emanare*, meaning "to flow out", and it is as the 93 current that life flows out of the world of *Atziluth. See Beast; Current; Khabs; Tetragrammaton; Worlds, Four.*

Aunnu

At Aunnu (Heliopolis or On), the mystery of Creation is described in its primeval aspect, and Atum-Ra is the name given to the hidden power that stands behind Creation. The name "Atum" means All and Nothing, representing the potentiality of the yet unformed universe. To exist as distinct from the *Nun*, Atum has to project himself—thus Atum "becomes". The Pyramid Texts describe this original act of Creation in the following terms:

"Hail Atum! Hail Khepri, he who becomes from himself! You culminate in this your name of 'Mound', you become in this your name of Scarab-Khepri."[93]

"Atum-Khepri, you culminate as mound, you raise yourself up as the Benu Bird from the ben-ben stone in the abode of the phoenix at Heliopolis."[94]

Atum thus surges out of the *Nun* as the Primordial Mound. Atum is then said by the Pyramid Texts to respectively spit out and expectorate Shu (Air and Space) and Tefnut (Fire), the first two divine principles. Alternatively he brings these into the world by masturbating and causing "the seed from the kidneys to come."[95]

In another version of the myth, Atum is said to have created himself by the projection of his own heart, and to bring forth with him eight elementary principles with which he becomes the Great Ennead of Heliopolis: Shu and Tefnut, then Geb the earth, Nuit the sky, and finally Osiris and Isis, Set and Nephthys, the entities of cyclic life and renewal, of death and rebirth. "None of them are separate from him," say the Pyramid Texts.[96]

Atum-Ra of Heliopolis is the carrier of the invisible fire or seed, the metaphysical cause of the first definition to arise from the *Nun*. He then brings forth from himself the nine divine principles (eight plus himself) that will order the Becoming.[97]

---

93 Pyramid Text, 1587.

94 Pyramid Text, 1652.

95 The kidneys here refer to the adrenals, the seat of the *Chiah, Chi* or vital energy.

96 Pyramid Text, 1655.

97 See Liber AL vel Legis, I: 15, "For I am perfect, being Not; and my number is nine by the fools; but with the just I am eight, and one in eight: Which is vital, for I am none indeed."

In the Pyramid Texts, this Great Ennead doubles, and then itself becomes a generative power: "The King comes forth from between the thighs of the two divine Nines." *See also: Hermopolis; Initiation—Egyptian centres of; Memphis; Thebes.*

Ba

The Egyptian name for the soul of man, and for the World Soul. The *Ba* is usually depicted as a bird with a human face. The goddesses Isis and Nephthys frequently took on this form, representing the dual nature of the soul. *See also Scarlet Woman; Soul.*

Babalon: See Scarlet Woman

Beast

The name "Beast" is particular to St. John's book of Revelation, in which it is given to the power who, with the "Scarlet Woman", rules over the material universe. Revelation refers to him as the beast "who was, and is not" (Rev. 17: 10), indicating that he is the power passing in and out of manifestation through the Abyss.

The word "Beast" is also related to the name of an ancient god called Bes, probably of either Semitic or African origin and represented by a dwarf. Bes, "the aged one who makes himself young again", was worshipped in early Egyptian dynasties; at some period under the New Kingdom he became identified with Horus the child, Hoor-paar-kraat. Little by little Bes was merged with other forms of the Sun God until at length he absorbed the qualities of Horus, Ra and Tum. As such, Bes also moved into close relationship with Hrumachis, the god of the Sphinx. The Beast, Bes, the Sphinx, Horus and other solar gods are all expressions of the solar, conscious and transformative power hidden in creation, animating it with a life that is cyclical.

By the XXVIth dynasty (the time of the Stele of Revealing named in Liber AL vel Legis), Bes was completely identified with Horus, with whom he shared the attribute of Lord of all the Typhonian Beasts.

Liber AL vel Legis reveals that the Beast is the manifestation of Hadit. Above the Abyss, the Beast is the supernal *Khabs*, the utterer of the Word. The Hebrew word for "beast" is *chi*, meaning also "alive; flowing". *Chi* is the root of the Hebrew *Chiah*, the name used in the Qabalah for the part of the human soul corresponding to the sphere of Chokmah and the world of Atziluth.

111

Through the "fall", the Beast becomes the spiritual counterpart of the natural soul. From him emanates the unseen breath, fragrance or intelligence that gives her life. He is the Holy Guardian Angel or *Khabs* hidden in creation, his power coiled and contained within the soul to sustain her life. Liber AL vel Legis describes the Beast as "ever a sun". As a sun, the Beast is the Word, the supreme cosmic power. He is the all-seeing divinity, the heart of the cosmos and the intelligence of the world. He is the transmitter of the 93 current of love under will, the blood of life, and as such, the appointer of life and death.

By analogy with atomic theory, the Beast operates as the proton does in the atom nucleus, and as the element carbon in terms of his function in the universal life cycle.

The carbon atom consists of 6 electrons, 6 protons and 6 neutrons—the three "sixes" which form the number of the Beast. *See also Atom; Carbon; Holy Guardian Angel; Khabs; Proton; Ruach; Scarlet Woman; Soul.*

Bes: See Beast

Briah

The name given to the creative world in the Qabalah. The world of Briah corresponds to the sphere of Binah on the Tree of Life, and to the first Hé of the classical formula of Tetragrammaton. The intelligence ruling over Briah is the Scarlet Woman in her celestial aspect. In Liber AL vel Legis, the world of Briah is referred to as the *Khu*. By Hebrew Qabalah, the number of Briah is 218. This is also the number of the Hebrew words for "moon" and "multitude", two ideas closely associated with the Scarlet Woman, and of the Hebrew word for "ether". The ether is the "upper air" of the Greeks, in other words, heaven. The word "ether" comes from the Greek *aithein*, meaning "burn, shine". This correspondence directly relates Briah to the magical body called the *Khu*, meaning the "shining one". *See Heaven; Khu; Scarlet Woman; Worlds, Four.*

Carbon

A non-metallic element whose atom includes six protons, six neutrons and six electrons. A key property of carbon is its ability to readily form covalent bonds with other atoms, filling the three empty orbitals of its outer or valence shell by sharing their electrons. Carbon thus forms a great variety of molecules.

Each carbon atom can share electrons with up to four different atoms, as well as combine with other carbon atoms. These properties allow carbon to act as the fundamental building block in molecules of organic, living matter. Carbon is present in all organic compounds, including DNA, the molecules carrying the genetic code of living organisms. Carbon is able to form more compounds than any other element except hydrogen. It is a key component of most materials made by plants and animals, including charcoal.

Graphite and diamond are made only of carbon atoms. Graphite is very soft and slippery, and diamond is the hardest substance known to man. In graphite, there are strong covalent bonds between carbon atoms in each layer. Only weak forces exist between layers, thus allowing the layers of carbon to slide over each other. On the other hand, in diamond each carbon atom is the same distance to each of its neighbouring carbon atoms. In this rigid network atoms cannot move. This explains why diamonds are so hard and have such a high melting point. The diamond structure consists of interlinking tetrahedrons of carbon. It is the strength of this infinite matrix of covalent bonds that make diamond the hardest natural material known. Each of the carbon atoms is in a tetrahedral environment, that is, each is bound to four other carbon atoms with all the angles being equal (109.47 degrees).

Carbon abounds in the Sun, stars, comets, and in the atmospheres of most planets. Like virtually all atoms, carbon atoms are made in the interior of stars during a supernova, an explosion of a star that emits vast amounts of energy. Atoms are thus built in thermonuclear reactions, high temperature events that fuse two nuclei together. Hydrogen atoms fuse together into a helium atom then helium atoms fuse into carbon. Carbon atoms can then fuse with helium into oxygen.

Chakra

The chakra is a Sanskrit word meaning, "wheel" or "circle". It is used to describe subtle energy centres through which the life force, *prana* or "93 current" is organised and distributed in the macrocosm and in the microcosm. Traditional Eastern occultism considers that there are six *chakras* in the human body; a seventh *chakra* is latent in uninitiated humans, and is placed outside the body, above the crown of the head. The *sahasrara chakra* flowers only when the dual forces within the soul obtain self-polarisation.

113

The *chakras* are thought by some to form the subtle counterpart of various endocrine glands. Like the endocrines, which secrete hormones or other products directly into the blood, the *chakras* secrete subtle essences or *kalas* directly into the etheric stream that supports the life of the spiritual bodies. The *chakras* form a passageway for the *Kundalini*, each *chakra* representing a type of consciousness. *See also Current; Kalas; Kundalini.*

Company of heaven: See Heaven

Chiah

In the Qabalah, the Chiah refers to one of the five parts of the human soul. The word Chiah comes from Chi, the Hebrew word for "life, living, flowing, beast or creature." The Chiah is the part of the soul corresponding to Chokmah on the Tree of Life, the sphere of "wisdom". Chokmah is the sphere of the Beast, the life-giving spirit and transmitter of the Word or True Will. The Chiah and the sphere of Chokmah correspond to the world of Atziluth. They are representations of the centre of consciousness called *Khabs* in Liber AL vel Legis. *See also Beast; Khabs; Soul.*

Circle, squaring of: See Pi

Crater Cup

A term used in the Bacchic Mysteries to refer to the metaphysical place of incarnation of the soul. The soul passes from eternity into time by descending into the Crater Cup, represented astrologically by the space enclosed between the zodiacal signs of Leo and Cancer.[98] In the twelve-fold life cycle of consciousness symbolised by the precession of the equinoxes, the Crater Cup corresponds to the "first hour". In the Crater Cup, the dual aspects of the soul co-exist in symbiosis. The purpose of the Great Work is to separate and differentiate these twin principles so that they may polarise each other, their synergetic interaction giving birth to a third principle transcending them both: an immortal star or *Khabs*, of which the Crater Cup becomes the *Khu. See also: Khabs; Khu.*

---

[98] See Liber AL vel Legis, I: 15, "For I am perfect, being Not; and my number is nine by the fools; but with the just I am eight, and one in eight: Which is vital, for I am none indeed."

Current (especially, 93 Current)

A current is a flow of energy between two opposite poles. The flow of this current creates a magnetic field. The "93 Current" of Thelema is the magical current flowing between Nuit and Hadit, and transmitted by the stars of Nuit, the *Khabs,* from which they emanate. The polarity between Hadit, who as movement is the Knower and knowledge itself, and Nuit, who as space is that which is known by Hadit, is the consciousness current weaving world appearance. *See also Magnetism.*

Da'ath: See Abyss

Electromagnetism: See Magnetism

Electron:[99]

Irreducible into anything smaller, electrons are thought to be one of the fundamental particles of the material universe. The electron carries a negative electric charge, and has a radius of zero. This absence of size means that it is not an extended object but simply a negatively charged point in space, and one of the lightest particles with a known mass. Electrons form a cloud around the nucleus of an atom and can behave as both particles and waves. Although all objects actually do so, it is only in a minute particle such as the electron that wave behaviour is measurable and important. As electrons behave like waves, they do not follow a specific path when orbiting around an atom nucleus. Instead they form negatively charged fields, regions called orbitals that correspond to the space in which the probability of finding the electron is greatest. The size and shape of an orbital varies depending on the energy of the electrons occupying it. *See also Atom; Electron Cloud; Neutron; Proton; Quantum Theory.*

Electron Cloud & Valence Shell

Orbiting electrons surround each atomic nucleus. These form an energy field called an electron cloud. The arrangement of electrons in this field, in which electrons orbit to form layers or shells, determines most of the atom's physical and chemical properties.

---

[99] JJ Thomson discovered the electron at Cambridge University, England, on 30 April 1897—while Aleister Crowley was in his third year at that university and where, according to his *Autohagiography*, he underwent the Trance of Sorrow.

The most significant factor influencing these properties is the configuration of the outermost shell of electrons, known as the atom's valence shell. This shell has to be full, that is, all the orbitals in the shell must have two electrons in order for the atom to be stable. An atom with a full valence shell will not react readily with other atoms, whereas an atom with an incomplete valence will chemically react with other atoms, exchanging or sharing electrons in order to fill its outer shell. Atoms seek to exist in the lowest energy state possible, and bond with other atoms to fill their outer shells because it requires less energy to exist in this bonded state.

Six gaseous elements—helium, neon, argon, krypton, xenon, and radon—have full valence shells and are often called the noble gases because they do not normally form compounds with other elements. A full valence shell, like that of atoms of noble gases, provides the lowest and most stable energy for an atom. Atoms that do not have a full valence shell try to lower their energy by filling up their valence shell. They can do this in several ways: Two atoms can share electrons to complete the valence shell of both atoms, an atom can shed or take on electrons to create a full valence shell, or a large number of atoms can share a common pool of electrons to complete their valence shells. *See also Atom; Atomic Bonding; Electron; Quantum Theory.*

Fall

The manifesting power of Hadit, who is 0, is equal to 2: the Scarlet Woman, life, and the Beast, the giver of life. In the eternity above the Abyss, the "two" are in perfect union. The current established by this supernal polarity is the 93 current, Knowledge or the serpent who breaks forth as the Abyss to divide infinity and create the world. The motion of the serpent brings about the shift in consciousness through which the Scarlet Woman and the Beast are precipitated into the Abyss, the knowledge of good and evil—the dualism that creates world appearance and their separation from each other.

The "fall" manifests the Scarlet Woman as Assiah, the material and visible world, the base of the Tree inhabited by man, demons, and the Qliphoth or shells of the dead. Coiled within her dwells the power of Hadit given unto her by the Beast, the *Kundalini* power that awakens her from the fall. The fall manifests the Beast as spirit, Yetzirah, the invisible, formative world hidden within the Scarlet Woman.

116

Divided from spirit by the fall, the Scarlet Woman loses the knowledge of the Word or True Will hidden within her. She can only become free from ignorance, sin and death by reuniting her consciousness to the word or Spirit concealed within her. *See Assiah; Beast; Hadit; Kundalini; Qliphoth; Scarlet Woman; Yetzirah.*

Hadit

Hadit is the complement of Nuit, whom he manifests as a celestial body or *Khu*. He is the movement begotten by infinite contraction. He is the utterer of Nuit's will and her "only son", called *Yechidah* in the Qabalah. Contracting in the body of Nuit, Hadit begets subtle centres of consciousness called *Khabs* or stars. In these he dwells as the life-giving Word or True Will. The radiations emanating from the *Khabs* transmit the Will or 93 current throughout the body of Nuit, the *Khu* that surrounds and sustains them. As movement, Hadit is pure force or thought, un-manifested. He is not; he is zero, yet at the same time he is the One Who Goes Forth.

Hadit is Life and the giver of Life, two principles that he manifests as the Scarlet Woman and the Beast. By Qabalistic Gematria Had is equal to 10 and therefore *Iota* or Yod, the secret seed or *bindu*. He is the Knower, and knowledge itself, the serpent whose motion precipitates life across the Abyss, the Creation or dualistic universe subject to life and death. As the begetter of world appearance, he is comparable to Hermes or Mercury in the higher sense. The Egyptians portrayed Hadit as a winged globe or sun disc, usually with erect uraeus serpents on either side. The wings show the mode of action or going forth. They convey movement upon the air or aethyr, thus introducing the idea of the life-giving breath of God or Gods (e.g., the Elohim mentioned in the opening verses of the biblical book of Genesis). The twin serpents are a symbol of dualism, the root of world appearance. They show the principle of generative power, the undulatory movement that begets time and spatial consciousness. The disc itself is identified with Ra, the sun god; it is a stellar symbol showing the cosmic nature of Hadit.

In exoteric Egyptian tales, Hadit portrays the heroic conqueror of the foes of Ra the sun god. Regarded esoterically, Hadit is the fire of life (or Occult Force, *Kundalini*, Serpent Power). Hadit is the transformer of the energy of the self otherwise bound up or restricted in the elemental nature of man. This he accomplishes through the mode of burning up and transfiguring the substance of the soul.

The awakening of the *Kundalini* in the non-initiate can give rise to an exaggeration of the ego complexes or aggregates of elemental force bound by the principle of attachment and limitation. (See the warning given by Hadit in Liber AL vel Legis, II: 26–27.)

By analogy with atomic theory, Hadit functions as the electron in the atom. The movement of the electron, known as its orbital, forms a quantum field or electron cloud analogous to the body of Nuit, the company of heaven or celestial *Khu*. *See also Atom; Current; Electron; Electron Cloud; Heaven; Khabs; Khu; Kundalini; Nuit; Yechidah.*

Hathoor: See Ahathoor

Heaven (and company of heaven)

Heaven is eternity, in contrast with the manifested universe that exists in perpetuity. It is the world "above" or macrocosm as opposed to the world "below" or microcosm. Hadit manifests Nuit as a living body, the company of heaven or celestial *Khu*, also called the "Scarlet Woman" in Liber AL vel Legis. The body of Nuit is the universe referred to as the world of Briah in the Holy Qabalah. The word "body" is here best understood as representing an intelligent formation of individual units gathered around a common function: manifesting the Word of Thelema, Nuit's Will. Such a unit or soul is referred to in the literature of the Gnosis variously as the Immortal Stone, Elixir of Life, the Quintessence or the Holy Graal. Liber AL vel Legis refers to it as a *Khabs*. By analogy with atomic theory, the body of Nuit is as the electron cloud. *See also Atom; Electron Cloud; Khabs; Khu; Scarlet Woman.*

Heliopolis: See Aunnu

Hermopolis

Hermopolis was the city of Hermes-Thoth the master of writing, numbers, measurement and time. It was the centre of instruction concerned with the description of the *Nun*, embodying its qualities and characteristics. Its creation story tells that the primal Ogdoad or Eight was formed from the body of a sacred child who issues forth from a lotus in the middle of the *Nun*, the indefinable substance that is the eternal source of the universe.

The *Nun* is envisaged as swampy mire; a seething primal cradle in which live four couples of serpents and frogs. Their names are Naun and Naunet, meaning both "the initial waters" and "inertia"; Heh and Hehet, meaning "spatial infinity"; Kek and Keket, "the darkness", and Amoun and Amounet, "that which is hidden". Niau and Niaut, "the void", sometimes replace Amoun and Amounet. The primordial Eight or Ogdoad as envisaged at Hermopolis form a single entity:

"You [the Eight] have made from your seed a germ [*bnn*], and you have instilled the seed in the lotus, by pouring the seminal fluid; you have deposited it in the *Nun*, condensed in a single form, and your inheritor takes his radiant birth under the aspect of a child."[100]

The child coming forth from the primordial lotus is Ra, the principle of light itself, whose fathers and mothers are the Eight. *See also Initiation, Egyptian Centres of; Ra; Thoth.*

Heru-ra-ha

The Egyptian double god whose twin aspects are Hoor-paar-kraat, the hidden universe, and Ra Hoor Khuit, the manifested universe. These twin aspects are similar to those embodied by the twins Set and Horus. Set and Horus (the Greek name for Heru) are sometimes represented (notably, at Aunnu) as the double god Heru-Set who like Heru-ra-ha, stands as a bridge across the Abyss, invisible and visible, dwelling in both eternity and in time. Heru-ra-ha (sometimes simply called Horus, although there are many Horus gods) is the god presiding over the Aeon or eternity in which dwell the souls of the "Imperishable Ones" who dwell forever in the body of Nuit. He is the guardian of the great threshold called the Abyss, and the Lord of the Last Judgement. Qabalistically, Heru-ra-ha adds to 418—see "Abrahadabra". *See also Aeon; Hoor-paar-kraat; Horus; Nuit; Ra Hoor Khuit; Set.*

Holy Guardian Angel

The Holy Guardian Angel is the spiritual counterpart or double of man's natural soul. From the point of view of the natural soul, i.e. human consciousness, the Angel is an objective being. Like the Egyptian god Set, he is always where consciousness is *not*.

---

[100] Edfu VI: 11–12, and Esna V: 263.

The manifestation or body of the Angel is what the ancient Egyptians called a *Khu;* his heart they called a *Khabs*. In the Four Worlds of the traditional Qabalah, the natural soul (known to the Egyptians as the *Ka*) is fallen and dwells in Assiah, the material world. The Angel rules over Yetzirah, the formative world. In Thelemic terms, the Angel's function is to receive the Word of the True Will and communicate it to the natural soul. For such communication to take place, the soul has to unite with the Angel in love under will—the magical formula of the Aeon of Horus given by Nuit in Liber AL vel Legis. Through this union, the Holy Guardian Angel consumes the life and substance of the natural soul or *Ka*. Thus the substance of the natural soul is transmuted into a body for the Holy Guardian Angel. This body or *Khu* is of the same essence as the body of Nuit, the company of heaven dwelling in the creative world, Briah. The Angel and the soul then form one body and one spirit, a *Khu* and a *Khabs*. Their substance has become identical to that of the celestial *Khabs* and *Khu*, the worlds of Briah and Atziluth, into whose lives they are able to pass to be born forever as a star in the company of heaven.

The Holy Guardian Angel is a poetic metaphor used by Iamblichus in his *De Mysteriis* for the being who is also referred to as the Augoeides (a Greek word derived from *Augos*, meaning "morning light"), Redeemer, the Messiah, the Alpha and Omega (personified as a Word made flesh) or simply, the Way. In Liber AL vel Legis the *Khu* and the *Khabs* are also referred to as the Scarlet Woman and the Beast. *See also Beast, Fall, Ka, Khabs, Khu, Heaven, and Scarlet Woman; Set.*

Hoor-paar-kraat

The Egyptian god of silence, the hidden aspect of the double god Heru-ra-ha and equivalent of the god Set. As latent and withdrawn, Hoor-paar-kraat is the dwarf-self, Holy Guardian Angel or *Khabs* who, when fertilised by the divine Word, comes to manifestation as his twin Ra Hoor Khuit. *See also Heru-ra-ha; Ra Hoor Khuit; Set.*

Horus

The Greek form of the Egyptian god named Heru or Hoor (Coptic), of which there are many forms. Horus generally represents consciousness moving across time and eternity, transcending death.

Horus is "that which rises up". As such, he is the Beast of Liber AL vel Legis. Each aspect of Horus corresponds to a particular phase in this great life cycle. The Egyptian name *HRU* means "countenance; face; sky; day". It is composed of the letter H, the letter of "breath", added to *RU*, "mouth", therefore meaning "the breath of Ra"—which was one of his many titles and attributes. The name Horus is related to the Greek word *hora*, meaning "season, hour". This relationship points to the changeable nature of consciousness embodied by Horus as it passes through the various stages of creation.

Horus is the twin of Set. He is the solar hero who represents consciousness emerging triumphant from the dark womb of his mother Nuit, Typhon or Draco. This victory comes after a long battle against the natural forces of dispersion embodied by the god Set, the opposer who perpetually attempts to slay Horus. Horus rules over both heaven and earth. His power is double, and its symbol is the Egyptian Sphinx. The Horus form most closely associated with the Sphinx is Hrumachis, one of the aspects of the god mentioned in Liber AL vel Legis. Other aspects of Horus are referred to as: Heru-ra-ha, Hoor-paar-kraat and Ra Hoor Khuit. Gods such as Tum, Ahathoor and Khephra are representations of the mutation of consciousness through the Horus cycle.

The ancient Egyptians attributed the god Horus to the planet Saturn. On the Tree of Life, Saturn corresponds to the sphere of Binah and the World of Briah, heaven. The Aeon of Horus thus represents the eternal life of the body of Nuit, the company of heaven. Saturn is the planet that rules the zodiacal sign of Aquarius; the Law of Thelema, which is the Law of the Aeon of Horus, was transmitted on the threshold of the Age of Aquarius. *See Aeon; Briah; Ahathoor; Heaven, Company of; Heru-ra-ha; Hoor-paar-kraat; Khephra; Nuit; Ra-hoor-khuit; Set; Sphinx; Thelema; Tum.*

Hrumachis (Harmachis; Hormaku)

The Greek name of the Egyptian god Heru-khuti, also known as "Horus of the two horizons", who represents the sun in his daily course across the sky from sunrise to sunset. Hrumachis is the god of the Sphinx, symbol of the duality of the manifested universe. As the god of the two horizons, Hrumachis is the embodiment of the principles of change, mutability and metamorphosis that characterise the life cycle of creation.

Various Horus gods such as Ahathoor and Ra Hoor Khuit are all forms of Hrumachis. Other Egyptian gods mentioned in Liber AL vel Legis such as Hoor-paar-kraat, Tum and Khephra, correspond to the invisible or un-manifested phases of the universal life cycle, or the frontiers thereof. The Horus god who stands as a bridge between the worlds is Heru-ra-ha, a double god whose twin aspects are Hoor-paar-kraat (the invisible universe) and Ra-hoor-khuit (the visible universe). The chief shrines of Hrumachis were at Aunnu (Heliopolis). *See also Ahathoor; Heru-ra-ha; Hoor-paar-kraat; Horus, Khephra; Ra-hoor-khuit; Sphinx.*

Initiation—Egyptian Centres of

Over the course of nearly three thousand years of history a myriad of initiation centres flourished in dynastic Egypt. Most were established along the Nile, which the Egyptians saw as a personification of the life current that sustains the universe. Five of these centres grew to be of particular importance in Egypt's history.

Starting from Upper Egypt, these are: Thebes, Abydos, Hermopolis, Memphis, and Aunnu. Of these five centres, Abydos was the most exoteric. It was the seat of large public performances of the mysteries, and a popular pilgrimage centre. It was at Abydos that many of the complex and esoteric themes of other centres were presented to the populace. The primary deities worshipped at Abydos were Osiris and Anubis, as well as the god Khentamentiu who became gradually absorbed by the cult of Osiris. Of greater esoteric significance were the mysteries of Thebes, Hermopolis, Memphis and Heliopolis (Aunnu). Uppermost and furthermost is Thebes (Karnak), the centre dedicated to the gods Atum, Mut, and their child Khonsu, the Moon.

The work of the priesthood of Thebes was particularly involved with the time cycles or *kalas* animating the life of the goddess worshipped there as the hippopotamus Apet. These cycles were understood to manifest the life of Amoun, the Hidden God dwelling inside the goddess. Thebes was therefore the centre most concerned with the passage of eternity into time, and with the life movement or current that results, including the great cycle known as the precession of the equinoxes.

Next down the course of the Nile is Hermopolis, the city of Hermes-Thoth. Thoth is the god ruling over the principle of creation by division and doubling, through which spirit acquires a shadow: matter.

The formation and transformation of matter was the focus of the work performed at the next centre down the Nile, Memphis. Memphis is situated at the crossroads between Upper and Lower Egypt. The material "double" was understood by the initiates of Memphis to be fashioned by the god Ptah-Sokar, the blacksmith who gives matter its form, and conversely transfigures matter back to spirit after death.

Following Memphis comes Aunnu, the "pillared city" where "the King comes forth from between the thighs of the two divine Nines". Aunnu (named Heliopolis by the Greeks) was located at the entrance of the Nile delta, across the river from the plateau of Giza where stands the Sphinx and the Pyramids. Aunnu was the physical location of the Primordial Mound, the place of birth of the Ever-becoming One and the point at which light enters the world. There, the Word was made flesh. *See also Aunnu, Hermopolis, Memphis, and Thebes.*

Ka

The Ka is man's astral double, the natural soul. The Egyptian hieroglyph of the *Ka* is two upraised hands and arms. The nature of the *Ka* is itself double. In Egyptian symbolism the gods Set and Horus represent the dual *Ka* of the Initiate or King, and stand on either side of him. In the non-initiate, the double *Ka* is housed— or imprisoned—by its feminine counterpart, *Khaibet,* which is often depicted as a shadow form of the person. Any man or woman has a *Ka* and a *Khaibet,* but without being polarised and thus liberated through Initiation, the *Ka* is subject to the desire-impulses arising from the shadow.

The *Khaibet,* or shadow, is itself bound up with the human identity or ego (which is that part of the shadow we think of as being 'ourselves'). The *Ka* double cannot therefore achieve its spiritual purpose, which is to offer its substance to the Holy Guardian Angel or *Khabs* for the formation of a *Khu,* by which the *Khabs* star can be "fixed". Through repeated union with the Angel, the *Khaibet,* which has no essential reality or substance, drops away like a shell (qlipha) or husk. The liberated dual principles Horus and Set then divide by the power of the sword of Zain. Through their polarity, they cause Hadit (the flame of life arising from darkness) to awaken and arise towards his Nuit (infinite bliss). *See also Holy Guardian Angel; Horus; Khabs; Khu; Qliphoth; Set.*

Kalas

A Sanskrit term indicative of the periodicity of the *prana* or breath of life. Literally, a *kala* is an interval of 96 seconds. There are 15 *kalas* to a *ghari* of twenty-four minutes duration; the *ghari* is itself the equivalent in time of a course of *tattwas* that are five elemental types of *prana*. The *prana* is what the Egyptians called the "breath of Ra", a subtle solar radiation which gives life and movement to things. In the Qabalah, this breath or life-giving spirit is called the Ruach.

The term *kalas* may be used in the wider sense of meaning subtle (i.e. non-material) rays, essences, colours or emanations that are comparable to the paths and colour scales of the Tree of Life of Qabalah. They are the radiations of Nuit, the subtle emanations radiating from the *Khabs* or star dwelling in her celestial body, the *Khu*. These emanations are also referred to as the 93 current. *See Current; Khabs; Khu; Ruach.*

Khabs

The Khabs is a centre of consciousness transmitting the 93 current throughout the *Khu*, the body or matrix that surrounds it. The *Khabs* is the "house" of Hadit. It refers to the being called the Holy Guardian Angel in the Western Tradition, and in Liber AL vel Legis the *Khabs* is also named the Beast. The *Khabs* corresponds to the Qabalistic world of Atziluth, and the sphere of Chokmah. Through the fall, the *Khabs* becomes the heart of the formative world of Yetzirah, and therefore of the Ruach also. It is the source of the spirit, intelligence or subtle fragrance animating creation.

Khabs is an Egyptian word for "star". More precisely, the word depicts a *portal* or doorway in space through which shines the light of a star. The metaphorical use of such a term in order to convey a highly abstract, intuitive concept was typical of the ancient Egyptian use of language. There is a subtle inference conveyed by the construction of this word. *Khabs* is the exact reverse or mirroring of the word *Sbak*. The latter depicts an opening or mouth that devours or consumes; it is a symbol of time.

The devouring gods were also constellations with astronomical and magical significance. The reversal of *Sbak* thus turns time backwards on itself. Through the breach in the circle of time an aperture in space is created through which is emitted the radiant light of a "star".

Sbak includes the word *Sba*, which has the meaning of a star in the literal sense. The star of the *Khabs* or Holy Guardian Angel is thus an inner doorway or aperture, a non-material means of ingress and egress between the worlds. *Abs*, the reverse of *Sba*, star, is an abyss, an emptiness or absence—the true state of the individual human consciousness. Thus the Word of the True Will is rendered in flesh or matter.

It can be seen that the word *Abs* is extended by the addition of the "k" of magick—the wheel of force of the letter Kaph whose number (20) is equal to the trump or annunciation of the birth of the Aeon of Horus. The word *Ab* also signifies the heart, a concept that the Egyptians understood as the seat of human consciousness. The heart or *Ab* is that which reveals the soul, the *Ba*, when consciousness is inwardly directed. *See also Holy Guardian Angel; Kalas; Khu; Ruach; Soul.*

Khephra

Ra, the sun god, in the form of a sacred beetle. The Egyptian creation myth tells that the sun god Ra emerged from the primeval mass of Nu (Nuit, infinite space, or the primordial void called *Nun*) under the form of Khephra. Khephra is called the "father of the gods" and the "self-produced"; he not only produced himself, but also begot, conceived and brought forth two deities, one male (Shu) and one female (Tefnut). As such, Khephra is the prototype of the androgynous god who begets creation through parthenogenesis.

From the state of living seed in the abyss of Nu, Khephra emerges in the form of the rising sun; conversely, Khephra is the symbol of the dead body containing a living germ about to pass from inertness to eternal life as an immortal body. Thus Khephra represents the transfiguration and resurrection of the body. The form of Ra with which Khephra is most closely allied is that of Hrumachis, the god of the Sphinx. *See Ra; Hrumachis; Nuit; Nun; Sphinx.*

Khu

An ancient Egyptian term, usually symbolised by a hieroglyph depicting a large heron, phoenix or other fabulous bird with a long, curved beak. The *Khu* is a magical body or matrix formed around a centre of consciousness called *Khabs*. The Word emanating from the *Khabs* is manifested and sustained by the *Khu* that contains it.

In Liber AL vel Legis the *Khu* refers to the "company of heaven", the celestial body of Nuit manifested by Hadit. As Life, the *Khu* is called the Scarlet Woman. In her dark or underworld aspect she is manifested as the material world, Assiah, and the natural soul, called Nephesch in the Qabalah. *See Khabs; Khu; Soul.*

Kundalini

The Sanskrit word for the magical, magnetic and life-giving power of Hadit transmitted to creation by the Beast, *Khabs* or Holy Guardian Angel. The *Kundalini* is also referred to as the Serpent Power and 93 current; its number is *Pi*. *See Beast; Current; Hadit; Holy Guardian Angel; Khabs; Pi.*

Maat

The Egyptian goddess of truth, justice, measure and balance. Her symbols are the feather and the scales. Maat presides over the universal equilibrium, and her law governs the Hall of Judgement, in which the hearts or souls of the deceased are weighed and assessed. The souls found justified at the Judgement are those whose lives have been true to the divine Word or Will.

The Egyptian Book of the Dead calls these souls *maa kheru*, meaning "he whose word is truth", a virtue attributed in Liber AL vel Legis to the prophets of Ankh-af-na-khonsu, "whose words are truth" (Liber AL vel Legis III: 37).

The utterer of the Word is the god Thoth, the male counterpart of Maat. The Book of the Dead states that Thoth and Maat stand one on each side of the boat of Ra (the sun god representing universal consciousness) and take an important part in directing the course of the boat.

Qabalistic correspondences are found for Maat both above and below the Abyss. Maat is attributed to the astrological sign of Libra. The sign of Libra corresponds to the path of Lamed, whose Tarot trump is called *Adjustment VIII*. The path stretches from Tiphereth to Geburah, that is, from the solar sphere of the heart, seat of the human will, to the sphere of Mars, seat of the Judgement.

The letter "L" (Lamed) stands for Maatian justice in the title of the Book of the Law of Thelema, Liber AL vel Legis. Venus rules the path of Libra on the Tree of Life, whose letter is Daleth and whose image is *The Empress IV*, stretching between the twin terminals of Chokmah and Binah above the Abyss.

The path of Daleth unites and equilibrates the primal polarity. It embodies the Maatian principles of justice, truth and balance, overseeing the Judgement or equilibration of the soul that takes place through the scales of Lamed. The close affinity between Maat as Justice and her consort Thoth as the Word is worth noting. *See Ankh-af-na-khonsu; Zain.*

Magick

Generally, the wisdom and science of the Magi—the wise men and women of old. The term is thus indicative of the Ancient Wisdom, handed down through the ages orally, and later inscribed in scriptures, talismans, hieroglyphics, stones and stars. Aleister Crowley rationally defined magick thus: "Magick is the Science and Art of causing Change to occur in conformity with Will."[101] *See also Holy Guardian Angel.*

Magnetism & Magnetic Field

Magnetism is a physical phenomenon produced by the motion of electric charges, which results in forces of attraction and repulsion between objects. Objects with opposite charges attract one another, whereas objects with identical charges repel each other. A magnetic field is a region in which the force of magnetism is active, around either a magnetic material or a moving electric charge. Magnetic objects such as a bar magnet or current-carrying wire produce a magnetic field that can influence other magnetic materials without physically contacting them.

One of the properties of a magnetic field is its direction, determined by the orientation of the electric current passing through it. This current manifests itself as magnetic flux lines, which form closed loops. The intensity of the magnetic field is directly proportional to the proximity between the flux lines, and magnetic objects within the field tend to align themselves along the magnetic flux lines. In addition to influencing magnetic materials, magnetic fields also influence charged particles moving through them. A charged particle moving through a magnetic field receives a force that is at right angles to its own velocity, and to the direction of the current within the field. This means that the path along which the particle moves within the field will be curved. *See also Atom; Atomic Forces; Current; Electron.*

---

[101] *Magick in Theory and Practice* by Aleister Crowley was first published in London in 1929.

Memphis

In the myths originating at Memphis, Creation is taken one stage further in the direction of matter. Ptah, the divine blacksmith, himself becomes the primordial fire and gives it substance. The archetypes that were enunciated by Atum at Heliopolis are here materialised by Ptah. The Shabaka Text (c. 710 BCE) enumerates Ptah's eight hypostases or qualities as "the *Neteru* who have come into existence in Ptah." He thus incarnates the primordial Eight, and then becomes Tatennen, "the earth which rises up"—an evocation of the Primordial Mound. The same text continues, "He who manifested himself has heart, he who manifested himself has tongue, in the likeness of Atum, is Ptah, the very ancient who gave life to all the *Neteru*." The heart and the tongue of Ptah "have power over" all the other members, since the tongue describes what the heart conceives. Thus Ptah recreates the Great Ennead (the nine divine principles that are brought forth from the secret seed or fire of Atum—nine including himself) and gives rise to all the qualities of things through the desire of his heart and the word of his tongue. The heart and tongue of Atum and Ptah are central to the Egyptian creation myth. They are referred to three times by Nuit in the first chapter of Liber AL vel Legis. It is said that the Ennead, which was the "seed and hand of Atum", becomes the "teeth and lips of Ptah" and gives a name to each thing, bringing it into existence.[102] Divine principles and qualities can now "enter into all species of things"—mineral, plant or animal—and become manifest through them. This is clearly an account of Creation by the Word. Ptah, together with Sekhmet and Nefertum, constitutes the first causal triad."[103]

At Memphis, Ptah and Sekhmet were said to have given birth to their son Nefertum, the primordial lotus emerging from the void. Like the Sun, Nefertum opens in the morning and closes at night. The name Ptah means "Creator". His was the Great Name of the *Neter* of Mennefer (Memphis), the capital of the dual Khemetic state for most of its history.[104] Ptah is depicted as a mummified man wearing a skullcap and bearing the symbols of life, power and stability (*ankh, was, djed*) in his unfettered arms, standing on the plinth that is part of Maat's hieroglyphic name.

---

[102] The Ennead is comparable to the nine spheres of the Tree of Life below Kether, where Kether is "none".

[103] Lucie Lamy, *Egyptian Mysteries*, Thames and Hudson Publications.

[104] Men-nefer means Justified Min, Min referring to Osiris in his ithyphallic form.

The plinth symbolises the straightedge used by stonemasons and architects.[105] Ptah is sometimes seen as a form of Atum, the Self-Created One, who effected creation through the actions of his heart (identified with Heru-Ur[106]) and his tongue (identified with Tahuti), and who "set all the *Neteru* in their places and gave all things the breath of life". As a creator, Ptah is more directly involved with the physical act of creating than either Atum-Ra, worshipped at Heliopolis, or Amoun, worshipped at Thebes. An earlier form of Ptah was Sokar. Ptah, Sokar and Osiris are often identified with each other, or can be seen to represent different aspects of one principle, that of death and resurrection. The name Sokar (Seker; Sokaris), means "Adorned One". This title is similar to the Greek word "Kristos", meaning "Anointed One", from whence is derived the name of Christ.

Both Christ and Sokar are representations of the Word made flesh, and of the cycle of renewal through birth, death and rebirth. An obscure name in its beginnings, Sokar is depicted as a hawk-headed mummified man and was originally Lord of both darkness and death (in the sense of inertia and inaction) in the region of Memphis and especially in Ankh-tawy ("Lady of Life", a name given to the large Memphite necropolis now known as Saqqara).

Sokar eventually came to be viewed as a mysterious, chthonic form of Ptah, and in very late periods was thrice syncretised to become Ptah-Sokar-Osiris, the penultimate lord of death, judgement and burial. The sacred boat upon which Sokar's icons were carried in procession (called *hennu*), is one of the earliest-mentioned of such boats in the Khemetic scriptures, and may have served as a model for later sacred barques. Sokar can be said to be the Hennu Boat itself. *See also Aunnu; Hermopolis; Initiation, Egyptian centres of; Thebes.*

Mentu

The Egyptian god of war, worshipped at Thebes as Mentu-Ra, a form of Amoun-Ra. *See also Thebes.*

---

[105] The skullcap worn by Ptah associates him with the skull or head worshipped in caves by the Calebites. The head in a cave is a representation of the incarnated Word or Word made flesh, a doctrine also associated with Christ. See John I: 14: "And the Word was made flesh, and dwelt among us."

[106] Heru-Ur is Horus the son of Nuit, the double god who looks both North and South.

Nephesch

In the Qabalah, the Nephesch represents one of the five parts of the human soul. On the Tree of Life it is attributed to the lunar sphere of Yesod and, in certain schemes, to the sphere of Malkuth. Nephesch is the Hebrew word for "to take breath", and generally for "soul" too, even though it most particularly refers to the soul of nature. The "breath" taken in by the soul is the Ruach, the wind, scent, fragrance or spirit hidden in creation and giving it life. In the Eastern tradition, the breath animating the soul is called *prana,* which is manifested in time by the *kalas. See also Kalas; Ruach; Scarlet Woman; Soul.*

Neschemah

In the Qabalah, the Neschemah represents one of the five parts of the human soul. On the Tree of Life the Neschemah is attributed to the sephira Binah, "Understanding". Neschemah means divine intelligence or intuition. The Neschemah is the consciousness attributed to the soul or Scarlet Woman in her celestial aspect. By contrast, the Nephesch represents the consciousness of the Scarlet Woman in the underworld (or post "fall").

Neutron

A subatomic particle of about the same mass as a proton, but without an electric charge. Neutrons are found in all atomic nuclei except those of ordinary hydrogen. Each neutron is made of three indivisible particles known as quarks. Without neutrons present in the atom nucleus, the repulsion among the positively charged protons would cause the nucleus to break apart or decay. *See also Atom; Atomic Forces; Electron; Proton; Quarks.*

Nuit

Nuit is infinite space and expansion. Hadit, her complement, manifests her as a celestial body. Hidden within her, he is infinite contraction and the utterer of her word. Hadit manifests Nuit as a celestial body called the *Khu,* in which the contraction of Hadit begets subtle centres of consciousness called *Khabs* or stars. The radiations emanating from the *Khabs* transmit Nuit's Word, the 93 current of love under will, throughout the *Khu* that surrounds and sustains them. Liber AL vel Legis also refers to the body of Nuit as the "company of heaven". Manifested as Life by Hadit, Nuit is called the "Scarlet Woman."

130

By Qabalistic *Gematria* Nuit adds to 75, equal to "stars and space", "the night". The "night" of Nuit corresponds to that which lies outside the "day" of ordinary human consciousness. She is infinite space in the sense of being beyond the enclosure of the rational human mind and the physical universe it perceives. *See also Hadit; Heaven; Khabs; Khu.*

Nun

The Egyptian word for the primordial void, called *Ain Soph* in the Qabalah.

Periodic Table of the Elements

A table of the chemical elements. The organisation of the periodic table is based on the atomic number of the elements, and reflects the way they fill their orbitals with electrons. There are 92 naturally occurring elements, ranging from hydrogen, which has atomic number 1, to uranium, whose atomic number is 92.

The periodic table also includes artificially created elements whose atomic numbers are higher than 92. Each column lists elements that share chemical properties, properties that depend on the arrangement of electrons in the orbitals of atoms. These elements have the same number of electrons in their valence shells. Different numbers of elements have similar valence shells, so the columns of the periodic table differ in height. The noble gases, whose valence shells are full, are all located in the rightmost column of the periodic table, labelled column 18. The noble gases all have full valence shells and are extremely stable. The column labelled 11 holds the elements copper, silver, and gold. These elements are metals that have partially filled valence shells and conduct electricity well. *See also Atom; Atomic Number; Electron Cloud & Valence Shell.*

Pi (π)

The sixteenth letter of the Greek alphabet, used in mathematics as symbol of the ratio between a circle's circumference and its diameter. *Pi* therefore represents an essential component of the formula of the squaring of the circle. This is expressed by the equation $\pi \times D = C$, or, conversely, $\pi = C/D$.

131

Metaphysically speaking, the squaring of the circle represents the Zayonic division of the circle of infinity by the polar opposition of twin principles, as well as the Maatian return of the twins to infinity by means of the application of the power of π to their synergetic interaction. The power of π is the power of the *Kundalini*, which fuses together soul and spirit, that is, the Scarlet Woman and the Beast, so they become a *Khabs* in a *Khu*.

Pi is a constant, infinite number. It may be approximately expressed by the ratio of 22/7, and is given to the sixth decimal place as 3.141593 by the riddle contained in Liber AL vel Legis III: 47. The solution of this riddle lies in the configuration of letters and numbers arranged in the grid that appears on page 16 of the book's manuscript. *See also Beast; Khabs; Khu; Kundalini; Maat; Scarlet Woman; Zain.*

Prana

The Sanskrit word for "breath", referring to the breath of life, fragrance or spirit animating creation. The movement of the *prana* is periodic, and the elements of this periodicity are called *kalas*. The breath of life is called *Ruach* in the Qabalah. *See Kalas; Ruach.*

Proton

A stable subatomic particle occurring in all atomic nuclei. The proton is made of three quarks and carries a positive charge of +1, exactly the opposite electric charge of the electron. In an electrically neutral atom the number of the protons and the number of electrons are equal, so that the positive and negative charges balance out to zero. While the proton is very small, it is fairly massive compared to the other particles that make up matter. A proton's mass is about 1,840 times the mass of an electron. *See also Atom; Electron; Neutron; Quarks.*

Qliphoth

Plural form of qlipha, "shell", "husk". The Qliphoth are the unbalanced forces of the universe, composed of units that are by themselves incomplete and therefore require union with other energies to find stability. The Qliphoth form the great dragon called Leviathan in the Bible, and whose name derives from the Hebrew word LVH meaning "to join, lend, borrow". It is by joining themselves to one another and exchanging energy that the Qliphoth find their stability.

By analogy with atomic theory, the Qliphoth behave as atoms bonding together due to their incomplete valence shells. Drawing energy from each other they are vampirical entities, and the redemption comes by means of finding stability in union with the eternal. The realm of the Qliphoth is the lunar or astral underworld of shadows, doubles, elemental spirits, man's natural soul and the shells of the dead—the underworld or 'fallen' aspect of the Scarlet Woman. In the Qabalah this material world is referred to as Assiah, which is cut off from the rest of the Tree of Life by the fall through which it has been divided from spirit.

The doctrine of the Qliphoth is closely related to that of the Egyptian *Ka* and *Khaibet*. The force sustaining the life of the Qliphoth is the power of Hadit transmitted to the human soul by the Beast. In the fallen universe, where man has freewill, this magical power is able to operate independently from the True Will. The forms that are ensouled by this magical power as a result of man's unregenerate desire body are illusory, mutable, perishable and vampirical. They imprison and obsess the soul who sustains them and drain away her energy, eventually leading her to dispersion. To be free from enslavement to the Qliphoth, the Initiate must master, release and transmute the life force they entrap. The Great Work is the work of transmuting the Qliphoth; the unbalanced forces of the natural soul must be organised through union with the word of the True Will. *See also Atom; Atomic Bonding; Beast; Fall; Hadit; Ka; Khu; Scarlet Woman; Electron Cloud & Valence Shell.*

Quantum Theory

Quantum theory describes matter as acting both as a particle and as a wave. This characteristic is called wave-particle duality. Wave-particle duality actually affects all particles and collections of particles, including protons, neutrons, and atoms themselves. But in terms of the structure of the atom, the wavelike nature of the electron is the most important. As waves, electrons have wavelengths and frequencies. The wavelength of an electron depends on the electron's energy. Since the energy of electrons is *kinetic* (energy related to motion), an electron's wavelength depends on how fast it is moving. The more energy an electron has, the shorter its wavelength is. Electron waves can interfere with each other, as waves along a shaken rope do. Because of the electron's wave-particle duality, the location of an electron within the atom's electron cloud can only be calculated as a probability.

The region of space that an electron occupies in an atom is called the electron's orbital. Similar orbitals constitute groups called shells, in which all electrons have similar levels of energy. Orbitals differ from each other in size, angular momentum, and magnetic properties. *See also Atom; Electron; Electron Cloud & Valence Shell; Proton; Neutron; Magnetism.*

Quarks

Protons and neutrons are made up of other, smaller particles called quarks that, with electrons, are considered to be the most fundamental particles in matter. Of the six different kinds of quarks known to date, two are found in protons and neutrons: up quarks and down quarks. Quarks are unique among all elementary particles in that they have electric charges that are fractions of the fundamental charge. All other particles have electric charges of zero or of whole multiples of the fundamental charge. Up quarks have electric charges of $+2/3$. Down quarks have charges of $-1/3$. A proton is made up of two up quarks and a down quark, so its electric charge is $2/3 + 2/3 - 1/3$, for a total charge of $+1$. A neutron is made up of an up quark and two down quarks, so its electric charge is $2/3 - 1/3 - 1/3$, for a net charge of zero. Physicists believe that quarks are true fundamental particles, so they have no internal structure and cannot be split into something smaller. *See also Atom; Electron; Neutron; Proton.*

Ra

The Egyptian sun god. Ra is self-created, and emerges from the *Nun* or primeval void in the form of Khephra, the sacred beetle. Ra is said to travel the infinite heavens in his boat of a million years, the Hennu boat. As such, Ra is as the *Khabs* within the *Khu*. *See also Khabs; Khephra; Khu; Nun.*

Ra Hoor Khuit

The Egyptian god of Force and Fire, that is, of manifestation. Ra Hoor Khuit is the projected aspect of the double god Heru-ra-ha, born of the interaction of Nuit and Hadit. His twin Hoor-paar-kraat is the hidden universe. Ra Hoor Khuit projects the True Will going forth from Nuit and Hadit into creation. He is a form of the god Hrumachis, the "god of the two horizons" representing the sun between sunrise and sunset, and whose symbol is the Sphinx. *See also Current; Hadit; Heru-ra-ha; Hoor-paar-kraat; Horus; Hrumachis; Nuit; Sphinx.*

Ruach

One of the five parts of the human soul in the Qabalah. On the Tree of Life the Ruach comprises the seven sephiroth from Chesed to Yesod, the latter being its point of contact with the part of the soul called Nephesch. Ruach is the Hebrew word for "breath; scent; fragrance". The word Ruach is used for "spirit", the breath of life forming and animating creation. In the Old Testament, this spirit is described as the primal force emerging from chaos: "And the earth was without form, and void; and darkness was upon the face of the deep. And the spirit of God moved upon the face of the waters" (Genesis 1: 2). The Ruach radiates out of the centre of consciousness called *Khabs* in Liber AL vel Legis, and permeates creation. *See also Current; Khabs; Nephesch; Soul.*

Scarlet Woman

The name "Scarlet Woman" originates from St. John's book of Revelation, in which it is given to the great prostitute Babylon (Revelation 17: 17–18). Together with the "Beast", she represents the force ruling the material universe. The name Babylon derives from the Hebrew word "Babel", meaning "anointed" as well as "mix, mingle and confuse". As manifested existence, she is multiplicity, the illusory *Maya* of Eastern mysticism. Her name is also related to the ancient Egyptian word for the soul, *Ba*. Her sacrament is bread, the visible manifestation of the spirit and the preserver of life which, having many grains in one substance, represents multiplicity.

Bread and cakes (see Liber AL vel Legis, III: 25) are the traditional sacrament of the goddess in most, if not all of her aspects. Revelation tells the allegorical story of her initiatory death, through which she is taken as bride by the Lamb and transfigured into the heavenly Jerusalem (or renewal of the Word at the spring equinox of Aries—see Revelation, 21). The nuptial feast that follows the hour of doom of the Scarlet Woman is a celebration of the soul's victory over death and world illusion, of her union with the eternal.

Aleister Crowley spelt the name "BABALON", as it is given in Elizabethan alchemist John Dee's Enochian Calls. The name is Chaldean for "Gate of the God", and Qabalistically adds to 156. This is also the number of Zion, the sacred mountain that the Initiate must ascend to triumph over the "word of Sin" that is "Restriction".

Liber AL vel Legis reveals that Hadit, the giver of life, manifests Nuit as the Scarlet Woman, the supernal *Khu* and creative world of Briah. In manifesting her, he manifests life, the body or matrix in which he comes into existence as the Beast, the supernal *Khabs* and world of Atziluth. In the Scarlet Woman "is all power given" (Liber AL vel Legis, I: 15). The power is that of Hadit, the serpent or 93 current animating the life of the Scarlet Woman and radiating from the *Khabs* contained within her.

Above the Abyss, the Scarlet Woman is the body of Nuit, the company of heaven, the intelligence referred to as Neschemah in the Qabalah. In her underworld aspect the Scarlet Woman is manifested as the great dragon, the material and visible world (Assiah) at the base of the Tree. Therein dwell man, demons, and the Qliphoth or shells of the dead. However, in earlier Sumerian depictions of the Scarlet Woman it is clear that the underworld was not then seen as a place of evil *ipso facto*—as it was in later times when scriptural interpretation became the sole means of conveying knowledge.

The descent of the Scarlet Woman into the underworld was originally not seen as a "fall from grace", but as a heroic act. By so doing, she is able to awaken the power of the Beast for the purposes of Initiation. So far as the 'sinful' nature of the Scarlet Woman is concerned, it is interesting to note that in Hebrew the word "sin" actually means "thorn" and "clay". Thorny plants such as the acacia or rose symbolise the horns of the crescent moon. The moon itself, like the clay shaped by the hands of the divine potter, is a symbol of the body and the natural soul. Liber AL vel Legis, I: 16, describes the Scarlet Woman as being "a moon"; as a moon, she is containment and receptivity, as well as the division into parts of cyclical, phasic existence. She is the placenta feeding the magical embryo or *Khabs.*

By analogy with atomic theory, the Scarlet Woman in the underworld is as the neutron in the atom nucleus; the celestial Scarlet Woman is as the electron cloud. *See also Atom; Beast; Briah; Electron Cloud; Khabs; Khu; Nephesch; Neschemah; Neutron; Soul.*

Set

The primordial god of the Egyptians, whose name has the meaning, "black". Set is the son of the great mother goddess Nuit-Typhon-Draco. He embodies the principles of dividing, cleaving, breaking, slaying and reversing.

Set is the means of ingress and egress between the worlds, and of passing backwards and forwards between time and eternity. Set is the "slayer of the real" who breaks the circle of infinity to beget creation. Conversely, Set moves through creation as the destroyer perpetually annihilating the forms he created out of chaos. His dwelling place is the desert, the burning and transforming expanse of the Abyss in which knowledge and the contents of mind turn to dust.

Set is the double; he is always where consciousness, embodied by his twin brother Horus, is not. Thus he drives consciousness forwards—which may mean backwards, depending on one's point of view! Through polarisation, Set both restores equilibrium where there is excess, and creates movement where there is inertia. He is the opposer, the accuser, the dark sun who presides over all that is opposite and "outside"—all that is other, alien, unseen and unexpected.

Set is the "sun of midnight" who is "ever a son" (Liber AL vel Legis III: 74). He is the beginning and the end, the Alpha and the Omega. As such he is the Lord of Initiation eternally moving consciousness beyond its own boundaries, whether towards or away from manifestation. Together, Set and Horus, the sky by night and the sky by day, form a ladder between heaven and earth. Appointer of life and death, Set is the Lord of Hell or Amenta. Evoker of the *nigredo*, he presides over the alchemical dross, the transmutation of which is the magical secret of the Great Work. The Setian forces of dispersion and change are the power that enables the cyclical renewal of the physical universe. Set is closely associated with Hadit and his manifestation, the Beast. The polarity of Set and Horus was known at Aunnu or On (Heliopolis) as the double god Heru-Set, whose attributes are similar to those of Heru-ra-ha. Aunnu was considered to be the birthplace of Horus, the Word. *See Heru-ra-ha; Hoor-paar-kraat; Horus; Ra Hoor Khuit.*

Sirius

Also known as Sothis (meaning "Soul of Isis" in Greek), or the Dog Star. This vast star is sometimes referred to as "the sun behind the sun", the source of the universe, the duplicator and renewer of time-cycles. Sirius is the star of Set, whose mother is Ahathoor. In ancient Egypt, Sirius was called the "Opener of the Year" as its rising corresponds to the rising of the Nile, the river whose waters bring life to the land and announces the renewal of life. *See also Ahathoor; Set.*

Soul

The Hebrew word for "soul" is Nephesch, meaning literally, "to take breath". In the Old Testament's book of Genesis, II: 7, the creation of the soul is described as follows:

"And the Lord God formed man of the dust of the ground, and breathed into his nostrils the breath of life; and man became a living soul."

The life-giving breath taken in by the soul is called the Ruach, a Hebrew word that means breath but also smell, scent or fragrance. The soul may thus be defined as matter animated by the divine breath or Word. In classical Greek, the soul is called *Psyche* that, like the Hebrew Nephesch, means the breath of life. The Greeks used the word *Psyche* to generally refer to everything in which there is life. They regarded the soul as the vital force that animates the body and shows itself in breathing. The meaning of the word *Psyche* thus covered the twin principles of force and form, the life-giving power of the divine breath or Ruach and the living creature or Nephesch it animates.

In biblical writings, the Nephesch is sometimes simply referred to as "the flesh". In Liber AL vel Legis, life and the life-giving power of the divine breath or Word are associated with Hadit, who declares that he is "Life and the giver of Life" (Liber AL vel Legis, II: 6). Hadit is the power hidden behind the life of the soul, whom he manifests as the Scarlet Woman. His life-giving power he manifests as the Beast.

Liber AL vel Legis also uses two Egyptian terms to refer to the matrix of life who takes in the divine breath and the source of this breath. These are called the *Khu* and the *Khabs.* Owing to the division of consciousness or "fall", these twin principles are themselves doubled. The *Khabs* and the *Khu* each dwell at once in eternity, where they are celestial and in perfect union, and in time, where they are separate from each other. The natural soul, called *Ka* by the ancient Egyptians, is granted freewill. Her life is individual and personal. She is the seat of the mind, will, appetites, desires and passions.

The life of the fallen soul is in nature, and is consequently mortal, mutable and perishable. To achieve Hadit, the natural soul must be reunited with her double that dwells in the immutable realm of spirit. Through magical incarnation her substance is transmuted; no longer bound to that which perishes, she becomes one with the word of her True Will.

The life cycle of the soul is summed up in the Qabalistic formula of Tetragrammaton. In the Qabalah, the soul of man is represented as having five parts: the *Yechidah, Chiah, Neschemah, Ruach* and *Nephesch. See also Beast; Chiah; Fall; Hadit; Yechidah; Khabs; Khu; Nephesch; Neschemah; Ruach; Scarlet Woman; Tetragrammaton.*

Sphinx

An ancient Egyptian stone figure situated on the plateau of Giza near the Pyramids. The Egyptian Sphinx has a lion's body and a human face, representing the dual nature of creation and the interaction of matter and spirit, of the bestial and the human. The lion and the man are symbols of the Kerubs of the astrological signs of Aquarius and Leo, the "Star" and the "Snake" of Liber AL vel Legis. These are the attributes of Nuit and Hadit, and of their manifestation, the Beast and Scarlet Woman, or the *Khabs* and the *Khu.*

The mystery of the Sphinx is that of the mutable, cyclical nature of the life of the universe and the human soul. This passes through four stages: creation in eternity; creation in the world of matter or time and space; death and dissolution of material existence or the "end of time", and finally, dissolution or return to eternity. This quaternary cycle emerges from the doubling of the primal polarity, Nuit and Hadit—a doubling that takes place through creation in matter. The universe, both unmanifest and manifested, thus comprises of four cardinal points, two of which are in eternity, and two in time. The cardinal points representing eternity are the North and the South, Aquarius and Leo, Nuit and Hadit manifested as the Beast or *Khabs,* and Scarlet Woman or *Khu.* Together they form the vertical axis of the cross—another symbol of the universe. The cardinal points representing time are the East and the West, the astrological signs of Taurus and Scorpio, the Beast and the Scarlet Woman in the underworld. These stand at each end of the horizon and form the horizontal axis of the Cross.

In classical mythology, the Sphinx is sometimes represented as a fourfold creature bearing the attributes of all four cardinal points. With a human face, the body of a bull, the feet of a lion and the wings of an eagle, this form of the Sphinx developed from the original image of the dual Egyptian Sphinx. The word "sphinx" itself comes from the Greek *sphingein,* a word that means, "to draw tight". Creation is a contraction of infinity.

Sphingein is also the root of the word "sphincter", which points to the relationship between the symbol of the Sphinx and the aperture through which eternity flows into time. This aperture is referred to in Liber AL vel Legis as the *Khabs* or Beast; in the Qabalah, it is referred to as the world of Atziluth and the sphere of Chokmah. One of the images of this metamorphic cycle of life, with its four cardinal points, is the circle of the Zodiac, symbol of the celestial *Khu*.

The Sphinx stands at the heart of its twelve signs, of which four are fixed: Leo, Aquarius, Taurus and Scorpio, the four aspects of the Sphinx. The number 12 lies at the basis of the ancient Egyptian description of the great life cycle of the universe, the macrocosm, and of its microcosmic counterpart, the human soul. The macrocosmic cycle was referred to as the Great Year, the precession of the equinoxes through which the earth's pole travels across twelve "months", the twelve astrological ages that together extend over a period of approximately 26,000 years. The microcosmic cycle of the soul was described as having twelve hours, the sixth hour being the halfway mark at which the soul begins her descent in the underworld. The ninth hour was that of the transmutation of the elements of the physical body, which was followed by the hour of judgement. It then took three more hours for the justified soul to rise from death and return to eternity.

The date at which the Egyptian Sphinx was built is speculative, but the constellation of Leo the Lion was rising in the direction which the Sphinx is facing around 10,000 BCE. At this time, the Sphinx—or its predecessor—would have been perfectly aligned with the polarity formed by Leo and Aquarius, or Hadit and Nuit.

Taking the starting point for the Sphinx from that "First Time" (as it was referred to by the ancient Egyptians), the astrological Age of Aquarius represents the 6th hour, the beginning of the descent into the underworld.

It is fitting that Liber AL vel Legis should have been transmitted when it was, as it contains the keys required by the soul for her triumphant emergence from the underworld so that she may pass into the eternal Aeon of Horus. Horus is the god of the Sphinx, his many forms corresponding to the various stages of transformation through which passes the life of the universe, and of the soul also. The name Horus is closely related to the Greek word *hora*, meaning "season, hour", the very principles of division into time. *See also Ankh-af-na-khonsu; Beast; Fall; Hadit; Horus; Khabs; Khu; Scarlet Woman.*

Spirit

The breath, intelligence or fragrance transmitting the Word to creation. The source of this intelligence is now understood as being Hadit, who manifests the 93 current. The transmitter of the 93 current is the Beast; the creation it animates is the Scarlet Woman or soul.

As a centre of consciousness whence emanates the spirit, the Beast is a *Khabs,* and the Holy Guardian Angel. As a body permeated by the spirit, the Scarlet Woman is the *Khu,* and the human soul. *See also Beast; Current; Hadit; Khabs; Khu; Scarlet Woman; Soul.*

Star

The star or *Khabs* is the true nature of every man and every woman, as revealed by Nuit in Liber AL vel Legis (I: 3). *See Khabs.*

Stele of Revealing

The funeral stone of a XXVIth dynasty Egyptian priest of the cult of Ankh-af-na-khonsu, who lived around the year 600 BCE. While a priest at Thebes, Ankh-af-na-khonsu received the revelation that is recorded on his funeral stone. This stele was exhibited at the Cairo museum at the time when Aleister and Rose Crowley were honeymooning in Egypt in 1904. Its exhibit number was 666, the number of the Beast of St. John's book of Revelation. Liber AL vel Legis directly refers to the Stele as "the Abomination of Desolation", a term borrowed from the Old Testament where it appears in Daniel's prophesy on the "end of time" (Daniel, 12). Jesus quoted the term later in the eschatological discourses recorded in the Gospels of St Matthew and Mark (Matthew, 24: 15, Mark, 13: 14). *See also Abyss; Ankh-af-na-khonsu; Beast; Heaven, company of.*

Tetragrammaton

In classical Qabalah, the four letters of the Hebrew name of God: Yod, Hé, Vav, Hé (YHVH, Yahweh or Jehovah). The Yod corresponds to the archetypal world, Atziluth, referred to as Father in the formula of Tetragrammaton. The first Hé corresponds to the creative world, Briah, referred to as the Mother. The Vav corresponds to the formative world, Yetzirah, referred to as the Son. The Hé final corresponds to the material world, Assiah, referred to as the Daughter.

The four principles embody the cardinal points of the cycle of consciousness and life of the soul through creation, fall, death and redemption. The Qabalistic formula of Tetragrammaton teaches that the fallen soul, the daughter, is to marry the son, the Holy Guardian Angel, to be placed back on the throne of her mother and reunited with her father.

The four letters corresponding to the elements are often used in contemporary Theurgic magical operations, as the biblical demiurge is incompatible with all other gods. Furthermore, the great lie of monotheism was that a heavenly father could give birth to all of creation. The Hermetic name of Tetragrammaton is thus *Shematah* (ShMATh): Shin (Atziluth), Mem (Briah), Aleph (Yetzirah) and Tav (Assiah). Shematah (ShMATh) means, "The Name", and is the word of IAO, the Beginning and the End (ATh). Shematah is the Immortal Essence realised in the flesh, and the perfected word of MAAT.

In Liber AL vel Legis, the four principles are seen to rest on the doubling of one original polarity, the Beast and the Scarlet Woman, or the *Khabs* and the *Khu*. The doubling comes about through descent into the underworld. On their emergence, the *Khabs* and *Khu* correspond to the Logos (Shin) and Matrix (Mem) of Tetragrammaton. Above the Abyss, the twin principles are in seamless union. Below the Abyss or in the underworld, the *Khabs* and *Khu* are the Holy Guardian Angel (Aleph) and the natural soul (Tav). Through the division of consciousness "for the chance of union" that is symbolised by the letter Zain, the two are in a state of separation, and are confounded by Eros and Thanatos. The Law of Thelema, "love under will", is the means of their reunion. Seen in this way, the formula of Tetragrammaton expresses the mystery of the Sphinx. *See also Assiah; Atziluth; Beast; Briah; Fall; Holy Guardian Angel; Khabs; Khu; Scarlet Woman; Sphinx; Thelema; Worlds, Four; Yetzirah; Zain.*

Thebes

The nature of the work that was performed by Initiates in Thebes is worth noting, as it sheds much light on some of the more obscure passages of Liber AL vel Legis. A group of temples at Thebes (Karnak) consecrated to the Theban Triad, Amoun, Mut and Khonsu, is called Apet-Sut. The word *sut* means place, and is also a root of the name Set.

The word *apet*, designating the female hippopotamus whose enormous belly symbolises the gestating womb, is derived from the root *ip*, meaning "to count", "to enumerate". Apet-Sut can thus be translated as "Enumerator of the Places", for the name implies that gestation is identified with counting. Numbers are thus seen as generative powers.

While Heliopolis and Memphis paid tribute to an Ennead of nine *Neteru* or gods, and Hermopolis to an Ogdoad of eight, Karnak replaced this with an unusual *fifteen Neteru*. Fifteen is a number of the primordial goddess and her magical child, Set-Typhon. More specifically, fifteen is descriptive of her *kalas* or emanations, which count the cyclical motion of the breath (*prana*) of life.

At Thebes, the Hidden God known there by the name of Amoun is represented by a walking figure, the vital breath that lives in all things, and moves by numbers.[107] Each one of the temples of Apet-Sut is consecrated to a particular entity or *Neter*, who is a principle or mode of action of the Hidden God.[108] The numbers conceal—and reveal—the *Neteru*.

Thebes is therefore the centre of instruction concerned with what later become known as the Qabalah. It is also the centre concerned with the precession of the equinoxes, and the "enumeration of the place" of Ra, the light of the Sun, around the Zodiac belt. The two principal deities of the Theban Triad, Amoun and Mut whose child is Khonsu, correspond astrologically to the signs of Aries and Libra (Amoun is often depicted as ram-headed, while Mut is associated with Maat and her scales). Aries and Libra are the two signs entered by the sun at the equinoxes. Khonsu carries the Eye of Ra, showing that, as the child of Amoun and Mut, he is the child of the enumeration of the cycle of the sun.

---

[107] The vital breath "moves by numbers" since it is periodical, cyclical, and rhythmical—its movement has a count. Such is the basis of the Qabalah (numbers are living entities), and of the science of the *kalas* that are the basis of cyclical time.

[108] The Hidden God was known at Thebes as Amoun, "The Concealed" or "Hidden Countenance". Amoun is hidden or concealed because he is invisible, below the horizon where the sun sets and where, in Egyptian symbolism, the sun god Ra enters the body of Nuit. The horizon is that which divides human or daytime consciousness from Nuit or night-time consciousness. The Hidden God is a term interchangeable with that of the Holy Guardian Angel.

It is therefore from Thebes that the precession of the equinoxes is declared. This is identical with the utterance of the Word that must become flesh. The Word made flesh is at the heart of the esoteric doctrine of ancient Egypt, and therefore of Liber AL vel Legis. *See also Ankh-af-na-khonsu; Initiation, Egyptian, centres of; Maat.*

Thebes—warrior lord of

The warrior lord of Thebes refers to a self-slain Theban priest of the cult of Ankh-af-na-khonsu. *See Ankh-af-na-khonsu.*

Thelema

Θελημα is the Greek word for "Will", and is the word of the law given by Nuit in Liber AL vel Legis. By Greek Qabalah, the number of Thelema is 93. Thelema is therefore identical to Agape (Αγαπη), spiritual love, which also has the value of 93. *See Aeon; Horus; Nuit.*

Thoth

The Egyptian god of writing and magick; the utterer of the Word, the intelligence of God and male counterpart of Maat. Thoth was known to the Greeks as Hermes, and to the Romans as Mercury. The ancient Egyptians attributed the god Set to the planet Mercury. This points to the close relationship between Set and Thoth, who gradually assimilated many of the attributes of Set as the latter became demonised. *See also Maat; Set.*

Tum

Originally, the first fully anthropomorphic god representing Ra as the sun in the East. Later, his position moved to the West and he came to represent the setting of Ra in the underworld—the reflection of Nuit's body. Tum thus became the god below the horizon, identical to Amoun the "Hidden God" worshipped at Thebes.

At Aunnu, Tum was Ra-Hoor when rising in the East, Ra-Tum when setting in the West, and the double head of the Hennu boat (the boat of Ra, also sometimes represented with Maat and Thoth directing its course). His earliest, primal form was that of Bes, the dwarf self or Holy Guardian Angel referred to as "the Beast" in Liber AL vel Legis. *See also Aunnu; Beast; Holy Guardian Angel; Ra; Thebes.*

Typhon

The Greek name for the multi-faceted god who perpetually destroys forms to bring about change in the universe. He appears in mythology under many names, including: Hadit, Set, Bes, or "the Beast". One of his symbols is the Egyptian Sphinx. Typhon is the son who manifests his mother, the primal Goddess who through him takes on any number of forms and aspects. The constellation named by the Egyptians as the "Thigh" (Ursa Major) was her stellar symbol or Word. The association between the constellation of Ursa Major and the star at the North Pole, at the Nuit-zenith—or northernmost extremity—is astronomically as well as magically significant. *See also Beast; Hadit; Nuit; Set; Sphinx.*

Valence Shell: See Electron Cloud

Worlds, Four

The Four Worlds of the Qabalah are, starting from the Supernals: Atziluth, the archetypal world; Briah, the creative world; Yetzirah, the formative world; Assiah, the material world. The mystery of the interaction of these four worlds is summed up in the Qabalistic formula of Tetragrammaton. *See also Assiah, Atziluth, Briah, Tetragrammaton and Yetzirah.*

Yechidah

In the Qabalah, the Yechidah refers to one of the five parts of the human soul, of whom it is the quintessence. On the Tree of Life, the Yechidah is attributed to the sphere of Kether. The Hebrew word Yechidah has the meaning, "one, only; only child". It refers to the only child of the great mother goddess Nuit: Hadit or Set, the divine Word. The title of "only begotten son" is also given to Jesus in the Gospels, such as in John I: 18 where John the Baptist says:

"No man hath seen God at any time; the only begotten son, which is in the bosom of the father, he hath declared him."

The word Yechidah derives from Yechid, meaning "united, joined", indicative of the inseparable nature of son and mother/father god. That is, of Hadit and Nuit. In the Eastern Tradition the Yechidah is called Atman, who is considered to be inseparable from the infinite god, Brahman.

145

Yetzirah

The Hebrew word for "formation" and the name of the formative world in the Qabalah. On the Tree of Life, Yetzirah corresponds to the seven sephiroth from Chesed to Yesod, that is, to the part of the soul called Ruach. Yetzirah also corresponds to the Vav of the classical formula of Tetragrammaton. The intelligence ruling over Yetzirah is the Holy Guardian Angel, the Beast or *Khabs.* By Hebrew Qabalah, the number of Yetzirah is 305. This is also the number of "a curving, bending", pointing to the relationship between the formative world of Yetzirah and the curvature of time and space that underlies the material world, Assiah.

The number 305 also corresponds to the Hebrew word for "Lamb", relating Yetzirah to the "Lamb of God", one of the titles given to Jesus Christ in the Gospel of St. John. The "Christ" or "anointed one" is the Holy Guardian Angel, the life-giving spirit.

Further numeric correspondences to Yetzirah are the Hebrew word for "dazzling with light", and the closing phrase of the 12th chapter of the book of Daniel, "the end of days". It is in this chapter of Daniel that appears the first biblical reference to the "Abomination of Desolation", a name given to the Stele of Revealing in Liber AL vel Legis. Yetzirah is the world which the soul must pass through to reach the end of time, cross the Abyss and enter into eternity. *See also Abyss; Beast; Heaven, Company of; Khabs; Ruach; Stele of Revealing; Tetragrammaton; Worlds, Four.*

Zain (or Zayin)

The name of the Hebrew letter corresponding to the number 7 and the Hebrew word for "sword". The sword is a symbol of the divine Word cutting through the circle of infinity—or non-duality—to beget creation. The existence of such creation depends on the dualistic nature of mind. The principle embodied by the sword is division and therefore doubling—a principle also associated with the Egyptian god Set. The name of Set is related to the word *Sept,* meaning "seven".

The correspondences to Zain are manifold. Beginning with the traditional Qabalistic attributions, Zain is the path of the Hermetic Tree of Life that crosses the Abyss from Tiphereth to Binah. The corresponding Tarot Atu is *The Lovers VI,* the twins representing the dualism between matter and spirit, man and Holy Guardian Angel. The path of Zain is attributed to the astrological sign of Gemini, itself ruled by the god Mercury.

Mercury is the Roman equivalent of the Egyptian god Thoth, the utterer of the divine Word and the male counterpart of Maat, the goddess of justice, truth and balance. Through the ages the god Set, who was identified with Mercury, became increasingly demonised in Egypt; his more positive attributes were gradually transferred to Thoth, whose totem animal is the Ibis.

Thoth is the male counterpart of Maat. Together, Thoth and Maat oversee the transmission of the divine Word or True Will. Zain, the path by which the Word begets duality across the Abyss, and Lamed, the Maatian path through which duality is maintained in equilibrium below the Abyss, are therefore complementary to each other. *See also Abyss; Maat; Set.*

Bibliography

MacGregor Mathers: *Kabbalah Unveiled*; *The Sacred Magic of Abramelin the Mage*.

G. R. S. Mead: *The Bacchic Mysteries*; *Thrice Greatest Hermes*.

Aleister Crowley: *Liber AL vel Legis, the Book of the Law*; *The Book of Thoth*; *Magick in Theory and Practice*; *Liber 777 & other Qabalistic writings*; *The Confessions of Aleister Crowley*; *The Equinox of the Gods*; *The Equinox: The Review of Scientific Illuminism*.

Kenneth Grant: *The Typhonian Trilogies* [Starfire Publications].

E. A. Wallis Budge: *Gods of the Egyptians*; *The Egyptian Book of the Dead*; *Egyptian Hieroglyphic Dictionary* [Dover Publications].

Lucie Lamy: *Egyptian Mysteries* [Thames & Hudson Publications].

Sir John Woodroffe ("Arthur Avalon"): *Serpent Power*.

Swami Vivekananda: *Jnana Yoga*; *Bhakti Yoga*; *Karma Yoga*.

Patanjali: *Yoga Sutras*.

The New Jerusalem Standard Bible.

The King James Bible (Standard and 1611 Bible and Apocrypha).

Revised Version Standard Catholic Edition Bible.

Lightning Source UK Ltd.
Milton Keynes UK
UKOW05f1831130817
307227UK00011B/323/P